THINKING
ON PURPOSE

A 15 Day Plan
TO A SMARTER LIFE

ISBN 978-0-9987167-3-2

Typesetting by Juan Gabriel Díaz R.
djuangabriel.myportfolio.com
Published by New Thinking Publications

NEW THINKING

PUBLICATIONS

DISCLAIMER
Please note that all information in this book is provided for
educational purposes only and should not be construed as, nor
replace medical or psychiatric advice.

The Society Of Neuro-Linguistic Programming™ Licensing Agreement

The Society of Neuro-Linguistic Programming™ - Richard Bandler is set up for the purpose of exerting quality control over those training programs, services and materials claiming to represent the model of Neuro-Linguistic Programming (NLP). The seal below indicates Society Certification and is usually advertised by Society approved Institutes.

When you purchase NLP products and seminars, ask to see this seal. This is your guarantee of quality.

It is common experience for many people when they are introduced to NLP and first begin to learn the technology, to be cautious and concerned with the possible uses and misuses.

As a protection for you and for those around you, the Society of NLP™ - Richard Bandler requires participants to sign a licensing agreement which guarantees that those licensed in this technology will use it with the highest integrity.

It is also a way to insure that all the trainings you attend are of the highest quality and that your trainers are updated and current with the constant evolution Neuro-Linguistic Programming and Design Human Engineering®, Neuro-Hypnotic Repatterning®, and other human technologies. Look for this seal.

The Society of NLP

NLP™ Seminars Group International, PO Box 424, Hopatcong, NJ 07843, USA
Tel: +1 (973) 770 3600
Website: www.purenlp.com
www.Society-of-NLP.com

PUBLISHERS NOTES

Welcome and thank you for purchasing Thinking on Purpose.

Bring your reading, learning experience to life. We have some members only content available at https://NewThinkingPublications.com. As an owner of this book you are entitled to a free membership. That membership entitles you access to interviews, chapter intros and outros.

Interlaced throughout our print publications are QR codes. Simply scan and visit. (free membership required)

Enjoy your learning...

DEDICATIONS

(from Dr Richard Bandler)

IN LOVING MEMORY OF MY MOTHER RUBY RYAN

(from Dr Glenda Bradstock)

TO MY PARENTS FOR TEACHING ME HOW TO BE HEALTHY AND
HAPPY

(from Owen Fitzpatrick)

TO MY PARENTS FOR THEIR SACRIFICES, UNWAVERING SUPPORT
AND ALL THE LOVE IN THE WORLD.

ACKNOWLEDGEMENTS

(FROM US ALL)

JOHN AND KATHLEEN LA VALLE for their wonderful support and friendship.

DOMINIC LUZI for his fantastic support and expertise in helping this book to come to fruition.

JANE PIKETT for her invaluable editing skills.

SHERRIE GRANA for her great help and advice with the book.

GILLIAN MCNAMARA-FOWLEY and DONAL KEARNEY for their wonderful support and suggestions from reading the book.

(FROM RICHARD)
Thanks to a lifetime and students and clients for all of the learnings I've gotten from them.

(FROM GLENDA)
Thanks to all my patients throughout the years that inspired me to continue learning to help more and more people.

(FROM OWEN)
To my incredible family, friends, colleagues, students and readers around the world for all their love, support and all I've learned from them. Also, to the Kessi's. Especially Will.

TABLE OF CONTENTS

HOW TO USE THIS BOOK

The way we have written this book makes it easier for you to create the kind of future that you desire. All too often, self-improvement books attempt to get you to make lots of big changes simultaneously. Here, we provide you with a 15-Day Plan to making your life wonderful.

This book is designed for you to start with the first section, and after that, take it a day at a time. The most important part of each chapter are the tasks that we set out for that day. We ask that you complete each task on each day. That way, after just over two weeks, you will find yourself having completed the book. Then the trick is to cycle through the 15 days over again as you continue to improve in all of the various skills that we cover. This book is a guide, so let it guide you as you experience the many life changes this 15-Day Plan brings. Why not give it a try and enjoy the new you?

INTRODUCTION

Your brain is a marvelous machine, capable of incredible feats; the single greatest reason we are the dominant organism on the planet. In particular, our capacity to learn from our experience and think ahead and plan is what has made the difference.

For example, when apes recognize fruit that's poison, they know not to eat it. They know that if they take a stick, they can beat something open and get what's inside, but they don't have little factories where they're creating perfect sticks to chop fruit, they're not planting orchards of fruit, they can't subdivide land and own property. What allowed us to do that is we made new things familiar – we adapted.

Those people who succeed more than others are the ones who adapt to new situations. If you want to sail across an ocean, you've got to have a ship. We made better and better ships and we went all the way around the planet. We've gone into the seas, we've gone into space, we are constantly adapting and expanding.

The universe is limitless, literally limitless. As we expand into this limitless universe, we're going to have to adapt faster and faster. This means we're going to have to get smarter and smarter. We're going to have to adapt, not through generations, but in a lifetime. We're going to have to adapt to technology, which means we have to learn geometrically. This requires that we Think on Purpose a lot more of the time.

A BRAVE NEW WORLD

What people call personal problems are nothing compared to what they're going to be really soon. Today, children are growing up learning how to use smartphones and tablets and they're learning to adapt faster than us. People who refuse to adapt are going to fall behind.

People who say, *"I don't have a clue about the Internet"* need to start learning about it. Publishing companies nowadays aren't doing well because of the downloads taking over from books. You have to become a part of the technology environment in which we live, and this has upsides and downsides. But we as human beings don't need to just survive with our technology because we have this marvelous machine called a brain.

Our brain feeds off energy; it's part of our living organism, not separate from us; it's part of our endemic nervous system and our sympathetic nervous system. Everything we eat, everything we breathe, everything we see, everything we hear creates this organism capable of manifesting the future that will allow us to fill the universe with life. If you look at this as our destiny, then you become an important part of it. Even if you live in the smallest town in the smallest country anywhere in the world, if you become the person who starts thinking this way, you will become a powerful force to be reckoned with.

This requires that instead of looking at personal problems and personal growth as the evolution of inner feelings, we take control of all of this and manifest greatness in all of us. We're spending too much time homogenizing society, making every kid in the second grade in every country in the world learn just X, and just Y. Instead, we have to teach people how to be learning machines; this requires they become problem solvers.

THE KEY TO ADAPTATION

The first problems that you have to solve are your own, because you're going to get new ones, and that's all there is to it. If you have overwhelming bad feelings about something that happened 12 years ago and it's consuming an hour a day of your life, well, that's a lot of hours over the next 20 years. You've got to be able to know how to think your way out of these things, because if you change the way you think, it will change the way you feel, and therefore change what you can do. Changing the way you think will determine what you can dream of, what you can imagine, what you can master.

As the world evolves at this rapid rate, we're all going to have to master new tasks, new situations; our children even more so and their children even more still. We have to become people who adapt mentally and become learning machines. We can't keep coming up against problems, throwing our hands up in the air and walking away; we can't just keep talking about the same old problems.

The big change made by Sigmund Freud, the founder of psycho-analysis, was the idea that the cure for mental illness, which was called *melancholia* at the time, was a talking cure (rather than hosing you down with cold water and all the other things that they had tried back then). Right now, we have to move up from the whole idea of mental illness and start to talk about *optimizing* the human brain so that it works maximally and perfectly and adapts to problems. This is what I call *Thinking on Purpose* and it's a learnable skill.

You have to learn to Think on Purpose because we won't just be solving problems, we will be exploring the edges of the universe – maybe not for you personally, but for those around us. The more of us who Think on Purpose, the more likely we are to survive as a species.

We're outgrowing this planet. You can say the problem is environmental change, but we're not going to be able to slow down population growth enough that we can all live here, otherwise we'd pollute ourselves to extinction. It's not climate change that's the biggest problem; the biggest problem is mental change. We're not creating enough human beings who are looking toward the future. We all have to start doing it.

Since the beginning of time, man has been looking up at the stars and wondering, *"What's up there?"* I believe the universe was formed and God's plan was very simple - He gave us everything and we're supposed to use everything, but first and foremost, He gave us our brain.

The reason you have eyes is to see, the reason you have a brain is to adjust what it is you see so you can live successfully. The secret to evolution – not just between species and between generations of a species, but evolution of a lifetime (which means getting smarter for human beings) – is to be able to adapt so that when something isn't working, you change what you're doing and find what does.

If you walk into a room and see a chair for the first time, you know what it's for and you know how to sit down. However, if you go and sit in it and it collapses underneath you, and it turns out it was a valuable antique that no one is supposed to sit on, that's another matter. I've walked into hotels where they have velvet ropes around the chairs next to the elevator, but if they're cleaning, they'll move the ropes. If you sit on one of those chairs and it collapses, you can either blame the chair or you can test the next chair you sit in; you can push it with your hand first to make sure it's not going to collapse. This is called adapting.

People are pretty good at the short-term stuff: they can try to open a door with a push, then when it doesn't work they pull and the door will open. However, when you get to the big things like making the moments of your life count, the measure of whether you're living successfully is how much time do you spend during a day feeling really good. The question is, how much time do you spend feeling really productive and achieving things versus worrying, being fearful, feeling bad and guilty about the past?

STARTING TO THINK DIFFERENTLY

People haven't made the distinction between thinking, under-standing, planning, and designing, and that thing that happens when people start working things out together. For example, business puts an emphasis on team-building so there will be group solutions to problems. They have advanced systems planning teams made up of people they have put together to be creative. However, they don't know how to design their minds so that they can work together to do that; they haven't found ways to modify thought, to optimize enough to put great thinkers together in different combinations and produce unexpected miracles.

This happened when people took great 19th Century innovators like Thomas Edison and Nikola Tesla and stuck them in the same place in New York. They even worked together in the same company, Edison Machine Works, for a spell. They were coming up with inventions every week. Then they told Edison there would be no use for electricity other than the teletype, but soon there were lightbulbs and heaters, vacuum cleaners and motors, generators and electric trains – electric everything. The number of electric things that exist now certainly make that statement the ultimate in stupidity.

People cannot see outside of what they believe; they don't take it as an act of faith that the universe is infinite. Part of being a problem-solver is believing that solutions exist and that they're not infinitely complex. Most things are, as the 20th Century thinker Moshé Feldenkrais described, the elusive obvious. We're just not looking at them from the right point of view, we're not simplifying them enough to understand.

In 1976, when illness hit the American Legion annual convention at a hotel in Philadelphia, investigators went in and used the same old methods to try to locate the bacteria. They took samples, put them in Petrie dishes and heated them up, but they couldn't find anything, so they didn't treat people and 29 died, even though legionnaires' disease is easily treatable with antibiotics.

Nobody thought to say, *"Well, let's give them antibiotics and see what happens."* They just let them die because they couldn't find the bacteria. It turns out the bacteria in this disease grow in the cold, not heat. Nobody said, *"What we're doing isn't working – we need to try something else."* There aren't formulas. Part of the way I've developed is when I get to where what I'm doing isn't achieving what I want, I flip it upside down. I do the opposite, in whatever form — even mathematically.

DOING IT WITH ENJOYMENT

When I was developing Neuro-Linguistic Programming (NLP), I was interested in a number of things. NLP is an attitude, methodology and technology of excellence. Part of what we do is understand people's strategies. What do they do inside their head to get the results they want?

When I was computing things about how people do things In their head, I literally stopped at one point and said, *"What would be the opposite of all of this?"* I asked, *"What would be the opposite of that mathematically?"* rather than using the principle of elegance. The principle of elegance is the process of trying to find the least number of things you need to do in order to achieve the best possible result.

That's when I came up with Design Human Engineering, where, instead of trying to do it as quickly and efficiently as possible, I started asking, *"How are we going to do this in a way where we can enjoy it while we're doing it?"*

I kept eliciting strategies that worked from people, yet the people weren't happy. They may have produced art, but they were miserable doing it. They may have written great music, but they were miserable doing it. Then they'd take drugs so they didn't feel bad. Even though the work accomplished what we'd set out for, I wanted to find out more instead of accepting the limitations; even though under the principles I had designed, it worked, it wasn't producing the right goals. I began to ask, *"Well, all of this is well and nice, but what isn't it doing? We're not producing happy, creative people who are having fun. We may be making people good at what they do, we may be making other people able to do what they do well, but it's one thing to be able to spell, and another to be able to enjoy the process."*

The truth is, when humans aren't enjoying things, they don't repeat them (unless they repeat them rigidly and unhappily, in which case the results aren't as exquisite as they could be). When you flip over something mathematically, when you start asking broader questions, when you start thinking instead of just remembering – this is how you do this, blah, blah, blah, 1, 2, 3, 4 – you start turning things around.

BUILDING FLEXIBILITY

I remember people arguing with me because originally the reframing technique had six steps. Reframing was a technique we developed to help people make a change in their life. It's not even a technique I use anymore, I see no point in it. We have much better tools now, but they still teach it. In other words, I'm telling them there's better stuff and they're going, *"Oh, but we have to have this old stuff."* It was basically designed as a trick - when people learned it and got results they got an endorphin rush. Then the next time I would teach it, I'd teach an eight-step reframing and people would get all upset about it. They'd go, *"Well, it should be six steps"* and I'd go, *"Yeah, but you can make eight. You can have other steps. It's made-up! You can make it up differently."*

It's like making an apple pie. You can throw a few cherries in it and it's still apple pie, you can throw in some cinnamon for flavor and it's still apple pie. If you get the result, maybe you can get the result with a little flair. I was shocked at how rigid people were.

I started understanding one of the most important things about the work I had done in identifying accessing cues, which told you how people were thinking. It kind of means you have to accept the idea of thinking in pictures, words, and feelings, because people wouldn't even admit it when I started.

I'd go in and say, *"Some people think by talking to themselves and some people think in just sounds and some people think in pictures; some construct pictures and some remember pictures, and some people think primarily with their feelings."* Everybody's got three strings to their bow. While everybody can do all of them, people technically have a primary system that they rely on. And people did research projects to try to disprove what I was saying. It was ludicrous, they said, this idea that your brain had pictures in it, because seeing things that weren't there had been defined as being crazy.

Your builder goes in and hallucinates something that's not there and either has it built or goes out and finds it; a civil engineer sees roads that aren't there and has people measure how much is going to be graveled. What's called hallucination in one place is called a job in another. Painters who don't see what they're going to paint ahead of time do modern art. My mother visualized everything that was going to be in a painting, drew it, could see the colors and the pictures, then filled it in from the picture. That's one way of painting, one way of drawing.

Another way of doing art is to make up a picture in your head, or to remember a picture from somewhere and paint it, or to look at something on the outside and copy it. They're all viable ways of doing art, yet when you talk to people who've been in therapy or you talk to psychiatrists, they'll think something is wrong.

Early on in the 1970s, when I would go and talk about this, psychiatrists would literally come up to me and say, *"So if you talk to yourself, you're not crazy?"* And I'd say, *"Is that what you tell yourself?"* I'd try to make a joke about it and they'd get very fidgety. Everybody talks to themselves, everybody goes inside their head and says, *"Oh shit." Some people go into their head and say, "I want an ice-cream,"* and that doesn't make them crazy. But if you went and told a doctor you were talking to yourself, he or she would say, *"Hmm, auditory hallucinations,"* and you might end up locked up or medicated. Early in my career, I discovered that this all went back to a time before radical new 20th Century therapists like Fritz Perls, founder of Gestalt Therapy.

THINKING

Years ago, there was philosophy, which was one big field, and people started breaking it into pieces. Psychology was the study of the mind, but it wasn't the study of thinking – that's a whole different thing. It wasn't the study of thinking, it wasn't the study of learning. Epistemology became the study of knowledge, but it wasn't the study of how you get it and how you test it and how you make sure it is working. *"I think, therefore I am"* is a nice idea as a proof about existence, but the question is: Do you say that to yourself? Do you make a picture of yourself being? Do you just have a feeling about it or do you do all three? In what order? For what purpose? If there's a different purpose, do you use a different order to get a different result? This demonstrates the difference between making decisions and remembering things.

If you're only born with two natural fears, then you have to learn all this other stuff. Obviously, people figured out a long time ago that part of the reason people have personal problems is crappy shit happens to them. Sometimes good shit happens to them and they get bad stuff from it. People end up being afraid of spiders when there are some poisonous spiders that are dangerous, but instead of learning which ones are dangerous, where they are on the planet and getting rid of dangerous spiders out of your house, people are afraid of every spider. They see one in the bathtub and they freak out.

Certainly, a piece of Kleenex will handle the situation adequately. How did they become afraid of that, afraid of trying things, afraid of all of these things? It's because the machine in the brain that learns goes haywire. It's not that haywire is bad, it's designed to make things familiar. That's what your brain's built to do, so that you don't have to repeat mistakes and you can repeat things that work.

They did an experiment with animals when I took my first psychology exam, Psychology 1A. Of course, when I took Psychology 1A and what they teach now should be profoundly different, but the real difference is all the talk about forms you have to fill out for the government. So, you're taking Psychology 1A and they're teaching you how to fill out paperwork as a social worker – that's part of the course. They're not talking about how people get better or how people get smarter.

THINKING VERSUS REMEMBERING

People go through the history of things, and they always start with the big guy. Certainly, the ideas of Sigmund Freud – the idea that you can have a talking cure for depression or a talking cure for feeling inadequate or a talking cure for melancholia (which later became mental diseases or hysteria or anxiety attacks) – were new at the time.

They gave these things names and tried to diagnose them medically. But instead of treating them medically, Freud thought that there could be talking cures. And he talked about the unconscious. People didn't know much about neurology at the time – they didn't know much about anything. With all the books that he wrote as he went along, there's one big underlying presupposition - something went wrong that has to be fixed.

Unfortunately, the people who went up against him, like Fritz Perls and the people who had created therapies that weren't just talking, all brought with them this same underlying presupposition - something went wrong that has to be fixed (rather than you learned something and over-learned it).

That presupposition demands that in order to go forward, you have to look backwards. So, all of the therapies that I've ever looked at do this thing where you have to look back, either overtly or metaphorically, interpreting dreams etc. It's all trying to get back to find where our learning went off the rails and became a malady, a complex.

They talk about having anxiety: You have anxiety because your father did X or you were attacked by a snake or you were bit by a shark or saw somebody bit by a shark, so you're afraid to swim. There are lots of cases where people fell into a river and they're afraid of swimming; they were a kid and they almost drowned. Their brain went over the top.

The movie Jaws came out in the 1970s and there were people who wouldn't swim in lakes in Kansas. That movie scared the piss out of a lot of people. There were people who came to me that wouldn't get in the bathtub; they wouldn't go to their own swimming pool. There wasn't going to be a shark there, but the minute their head was sticking up out of the water, it triggered the feeling they had in the movie that frightened them.

Rather than their brain reassessing at that moment and thinking, it just continued to remember, and it made the memory stronger every time they thought about it, to the point where looking at the pool scared them, looking at a lake scared them.

Even thinking about spiders was terrifying, but most people are not afraid of the actual object, they're afraid of thinking about the object – it's the thought that scares them. I bring people in and tell them there's a giant spider in the next room, that I'm going to bring it out, and they're going to hold it in their hand. Whether there's a spider or not, they become afraid. Then, when they're freaking out, I point out that there's no spider. They go, *"Well, you said there's one in the next room,"* and I go, *"Well, I could be lying."*

It's Schrödinger's Cat – really! Erwin Schrödinger, the Austrian quantum physicist, came up with this hypothetical experiment in which a cat is placed in a sealed box with a radioactive sample, a Geiger counter and a bottle of poison. If the Geiger counter detects that the radioactive material has decayed, it will trigger the smashing of the bottle of poison and the cat will be killed. There is no way of knowing whether or not the radioactive material has decayed enough to smash the bottle of poison. Thus, until we actually open the box the cat is both dead and alive at the same time. There are two possible realities happening. I always loved this because of the question, is the cat alive? Is it dead? You don't know until you look in the box.

Back to the spider - is there the spider there? It doesn't matter because you're already afraid. This means the fear doesn't come from the spider, the fear comes from thinking about it. So, the way you are thinking is producing the fear. But even then, it's not really the way you're thinking, it's the way you're remembering because you learned to do this.

You amplified it because our brain is designed to generalize. You learn what a chair is, and anyone seeing something that kind of looks like a chair has to generalize and say, *"Well, that's close enough. It is a chair. It's an object that I can sit in."* Some chairs don't look at all like chairs, but you still know what they're supposed to be and what they're supposed to do. I remember the first time I saw one of those really modern, avant-garde chaise longue things. I remember looking at it and going, *"What the hell is that? It's to sit in next to the pool! You don't fall through those things?"* No, it's just like a chair – well, it isn't at all like a chair, but it's close enough.

The learned helplessness experiment in psychology that always struck me as really important is really goofy. They made a **C** and they made a **O**, and if the animal touched the **C**, it got a food reward, if it touched the **O**, it got shocked. And so, after a while, the animal figured it out: If you run up and hit the **C** button - bang! - it was fine. But then they started to make the **C** a little bigger, and opening up the **O**, and at a certain point, you can't tell one from the other.

The animals literally went crazy because it was harder and harder to know which button to touch to get the reward. That's the point when subjects started to go crazy and wouldn't touch either of them. No experimentation, no learning, no risk-taking – they both looked too close to the **C**. If the C and the **O** aren't different enough, and people can't tell them apart - that place in the middle where you can't make the decision - you either become a thinker who finds a way to find out and a way to reduce fear by testing, or you just become immobilized, which is what happened to most of the animals. They didn't *do anything*, they worried, they freaked out, and they literally starved to death rather than figure it out.

They told me about that experiment in college and I remember thinking that was a really mean thing to do. Years later, I thought back and said, *"Well, they did the experiment, but they missed the point of it."* The point is almost everything in life is like that for us people. There never were **Os** and **Cs** to start with, right? So for some things, we make everything into **Os**: every spider is a bad, scary spider; every snake will bite you and kill you.

Some people can't get in the car and drive because they could be killed; some people won't get in an elevator – which it turns out is the safest form of transportation (fewer people die riding in elevators than walking). More people slip on the linoleum walking up to an elevator than die in elevators. Oddly enough, somebody keeps track of this kind of stuff.

It's not based on experience. It's funny, people will get in a plane and then be afraid to fly. Some people are so afraid to fly that they won't get in the plane. I've been in airplanes where they've sat somebody next to me who's freaking out before they even start the engines, before we're even moving.

I've had people sit next to me who put blankets over their heads so they couldn't see they were flying - like they wouldn't know! I'd literally say to them, *"Are you okay?"* and they'd go, *"I'm fine. I'll be okay once we're in the air."* And I'm going, *"What kind of sense does that make? 'As soon as we leave the ground, then I'll be okay'?"* I've had some of them who weren't okay; they'd stare at the wing, watch it going up and down and say, *"That could actually break off."* And I'd go, *"Yeah, and we could be shot out of the sky by a Martian,"* which is plausible, but unlikely.

Planes do crash, but once you're in them, you really have no control – that's up to the pilot. You just have to hope he knows what he's doing and enjoy the flight. If you crash, you'll know when it's time to worry. It's not going to keep the plane in the air. If it did, planes would all be safe, but the fact is most people don't make the distinction between remembering and thinking. Psychology doesn't make the distinction between the past and the future - where you're actually going.

To me, we haven't looked at learning as anything other than *What. What* did you learn? *What* was wrong with *what* you learned? Where did you go off the right track and become a fucked-up person? Psychology is looking for the malady. Even in education, when I started studying education in college, it was all diagnosis, it was all about learning disabilities - *"They've got attention deficit disorder blah blah blah."* It wasn't *"How do you acquire this information and make good decisions about what to do with it?"* Nobody's talking about that.

Nobody's saying, *"How does the person who does this well do it well?"* When NLP came along, the anthropologist and social scientist Gregory Bateson, who helped me immensely and who I studied and learned a lot from, kept saying to me that it was paradoxical that you can't use a pattern to teach a pattern, because there's *Learning 1*: learning to name things, *Learning 2*: learning to generalize from that name to other things (so you're not only naming this *computer*, you can call others *computer* and know what those computers are doing), and *Learning 3*: learning how to design and build machines that do things.

A MORE INTELLIGENT LEARNING MACHINE

I remember early on, I got a computer for my secretary. She was doing things and I thought, *"What's wrong with this machine is it doesn't teach my secretary how to be a secretary. We should have a machine where the only programs in it are those that teach her what she needs to know to be a good secretary. It should teach her how to type, it should teach her if she's making mistakes typing, it should find out if it's her emotional stuff getting in her way and all those different things. If the phone rings, it should know and go answer the phone and put a message on it. It should be making the stuff that makes it so after she uses it for a while, she could probably get by on a typewriter and be a good secretary."*

In those days, computers didn't do a hell of a lot more than a typewriter – but they should have. Now we have apps. But we're still asking people to use these apps and to make these distinctions and to log things in. Now, every time they give a pill to my mother, it gets computerized in so every work station knows she's taken the pill - that way you don't get one twice. That's good use of a machine that networks, if you ask me.

However, I go in and ask her, *"Did you get this medication?"* and she'll go, *"No,"* because the app doesn't remind people what they've had. It should. And then it should red-flag any change to the pattern - *"Is this the way it's supposed to be?"* – so that there's a check system; it should check with the doctor and check with the nurse, because bad things can happen - you can give people the wrong medication.

Machines are supposed to work for us. When they talk about a singularity of thought, they're talking about machines getting to the point where they make these decisions. They should be presenting them to us. These are tools, because it's always going to boil down to who designed it and how well they were thinking when they designed it.

Whoever designs a program, it's a representation of their mind on paper. If they learn to do something well and put it in an app, hopefully it will install in people so after a while, they wouldn't need it. Your address book app should be teaching you how to remember addresses; it shouldn't just be keeping them for you, it should make it so when you think about the address, it comes to your head as rapidly as you can find it on your phone.

We're not using tools to make us smarter. So, are we going to make the tools smarter than we are, or are we going to start evolving? And in order to start evolving, we have to stop diagnosing ourselves by our faults and the things we lack and start modifying ourselves by what we want.

This requires a different mindset than the whole field of psychology has had. You have to stop looking backwards and we have to start looking forwards. We have to get to the point where the best thing about the past is that it's over.

Everything that works from the past, we get to take with us, and everything that doesn't work, we find a better way to do it in our mind. Somebody's mind might have a better way of doing it, or we could make one up. Even better, the stuff we actually do well, maybe we can do even better and get better results, and better kinds of results.

It's the result when psychiatrists gave people medication for manic depression and chopped off all the highs and all the lows. Well, they were more manageable, but most manic depressives hated the medication because they felt foggy, they didn't feel alive. They lost the good feelings they'd had from those states and didn't learn to control their states. So when they got manic, they got too manic, and if they went off the medication, they'd still be just as stupid as they were before.

We're going to have to make a decision to make ourselves smarter (not just patients, but everybody – every single one of us). And the only way we can do that is by learning to Think on Purpose.

LEARNING TO THINK ON PURPOSE

When we say the term *Thinking on Purpose*, it's the "on purpose" part of it that matters the most. If you just *think*, you can think yourself into problems. It's really easy. For example, you see a little bug and you think it *could* be a big bug, so you make a picture of a huge bug in your head to the point where it frightens you.

Then you remember it, you start remembering that bugs can be scary. Next thing you know, when you see a little bug, you see a big picture and you keep remembering it, and the more you remember it, the more you scare yourself. Suddenly you're afraid of bugs, or spiders, or snakes, or public speaking.

You think somebody could cheat on you and you imagine it and feel as if they did and you remember that feeling, then every time they do something you start acting it as if it was real. You really can think yourself into problems. That's why you need to Think on Purpose rather than as a reaction to something.

Of course, there are lots of bad things that could happen and some things you need to prepare for, that's why some people buy car insurance. You could have an accident. If you back your car into somebody, you obviously didn't do it on purpose, but you also don't think every time you back up your car, you're going to hit something. If you did that, you'd never drive.

The more you immobilize yourself by thinking bad thoughts and remembering them (or worse, construct images in your mind worse than life itself) and acting as if those things are *real*, the more trouble you will create for yourself. Most phobias, fears, and anxieties that we deal with are people who have taken something that is real and blown it out of proportion in their mind. If you blow something up and then remember the blown-up version rather than the real thing, you're going to have problems.

The purpose of thinking is to think your way beyond difficulty. When people come in and they're thinking of a giant spider in their head so they're afraid of little tiny ones, they have to take that picture and shrink it down, make it black and white, or do something other than what they're doing so they're not afraid.

We need to use our thinking processes for what they were made for and we need to use our remembering process for what they were made for. Remembering can be a good thing or a bad thing.

I mean, if you remember things that aren't real as if they are real, you can scare yourself, you can disappoint yourself, you can immobilize yourself. If you remember how you were taught to spell and you were taught to spell phonetically, you'll always be a bad speller; you'll be sounding out words in a language like English that has silent letters. You won't do it accurately.

On the other hand, if you use *remembering* for what it was made for and you practice it and think of it as a skill, you'll be much better off. It's about thinking of it as a skill, an important skill. We're not just talking about cognitive thinking. It's about everything we do, every day. It's our conscious mind interfacing with our neurology, it affects how we feel and how much stress we're in.

People who have really high levels of stress start running things in the back of their mind over and over again. It's bad enough you're in a stressful situation once, but to keep playing it over and over in your head, and running variations of it in your head, so you actually create more stress than the situation did, is far worse.

I've had people come to see me and they're still having arguments with their mother 20 years after her death and stressing about it! I remember when I started with clients in my twenties. I didn't grow up with a family history where I spent a lot of time with my parents; my parents were working so I spent a lot of time by myself. People would come in and go, *"I argue with my mother every day,"* and I'd go, *"Yeah?"*

I'd be talking to someone 60 years old and who'd been in therapy for 20 years. I'd ask them:

"You're still arguing with your mother?"

"Yes, every day."

"Does she live with you?"

"Well no, my mother died years ago."

"What do you mean you're arguing with her?"

"Well, you know, I hear the arguments in my head. When I go to do something, I can hear my mother criticize me."

"Really?"

So, if she did criticize them, then they're remembering it; if she didn't criticize them for this particular thing, they're constructing her voice over and over again. They're thinking themselves into more pain. They remember the criticism and they play it over and over again. Our ability to create things in our head is a good thing, but it also can be crazy crippling.

Unfortunately, often people find it easier to remember horrific cases of things that happened, even when they are rare. The brain tends to focus more on disasters and people think they're more likely to die in plane crashes or being eaten by a shark than whatever is likely to happen. Our brains can create terrifying scenarios and exaggerate things in a way that doesn't work for us.

Part of it is there's a reason to start thinking, because if enough people start thinking, it's going to hit a point where thinking together produces more than thinking individually. This is what happens when you bring groups of people together in the same place, there's a certain kind of synchronicity – even musically, like when there were so many people in San Francisco, all making great music at the same time in the same place, an explosion of creativity in every way, shape, and form.

The same thing has happened at certain times in New York and it's happened throughout history. We have a whole lot of talented people together influencing each other. Fortunately, that group of people has always been small. With the advent of the Ethernet in the 1970s, a lot of brilliant people started being able to talk to each other. And then it got taken over by the Internet, which of course watered everything down. I'm sure the world's most famous physicist Stephen Hawking had a fan page, but it was hard for him to meet people on there who weren't trying to find him for the wrong reasons. It's one thing when you have three or four great artists playing off each other; it's another when someone is coming to tag onto their reputation.

There are points of singularity in history when things have evolved, but we haven't hit the one where consciousness has done that. We keep talking about it happening to machines – at a certain point of time, consciousness is going to hit a point in machines when they can *think for themselves*; they will become conscious – but the truth is, to a certain degree, this hasn't happened with people yet.

HOW HUMOR HELPS US THINK

The biggest inoculation against our mental problems is a sense of humor. The intensity of the feelings when the movie Jaws came out reached ludicrous levels. There were companies which sold diving equipment and did $30 million one year, then $100,000 the next because people wouldn't go in the ocean. It didn't suddenly become more dangerous, it's just people weren't taking diving lessons because they saw this movie. Oddly enough, people who weren't anywhere near the ocean were thinking about it, scaring the crap out of themselves, and not swimming in pools at night.

People were not going into creeks and reservoirs with no sharks in them, because when they saw water, their adrenaline response to the movie linked water with sharks. Post-Traumatic Stress Disorder (PTSD) is not just a response to reality, it's not just that you were in a war zone or a car accident; when people hear about horrific things and see it on the news, they go in and imagine being in it, they don't play it life-size in their brain, they play it larger than life. If they build really strong responses to it internally, those strong responses have a tendency to do it more, to exaggerate more. When you're told about something or you see it on TV or you see it in the movies or you have it happen in real life, the more adrenaline, the more shocking that something is.

Some of the guys who came back from the Vietnam War were literally re-living the experiences they had; some of them they actually had, and some of them weren't real. They had trouble telling the things that really happened over there from the ones that didn't, which they imagined could have. Because the experiences were both so intense, so overwhelming, and these guys spent so much time in situations of danger, their adrenaline levels ran higher than they should.

We're designed to experience stress about once a month, which means our nervous system isn't prepared for modern life. When our cellphone goes off or we're late for something, we run much more adrenaline through our system than it's designed for. You can customize yourself, but if you don't counter-balance that with humor, you're in trouble. That's why it's the tool I use to get everybody through it.

When I talk to a guy years after Vietnam and he's having nightmares about it and talking to everybody about it, going to support groups where they re-live it together, it doesn't get him to get to the point where his brain is going, *"This is over."* He keeps these things big and intense, and when he comes back, life doesn't feel real to him because it's not as intense. People like him don't come back and turn up the pictures of enjoyment. When things are in the past, you have to shrink them down and push them away; it's mechanically what you do in your brain, it reduces the level of these things.

I have to get people to laugh about it first; endorphins and oxytocin are what is needed. All the neurotransmitters that are released when you look at something, when you see yourself in a situation, when you see yourself walking around in the middle of the night in a suburb of California – which is perfectly safe – feeling like you're still in Vietnam. If you can't look at that and laugh a little bit, you're in deep trouble.

When psychologists try to get people to re-live this stuff, they're not really helping because the problem is the person is already re-living it. And sometimes they make it worse than when they were actually there, which raises the adrenaline that is connected with those past pictures. Instead of getting people to look forward to good things, they're looking back, they're running away from bad things. Our nervous system is designed to make things familiar and it will make anything familiar if you allow it.

When you're making things familiar that make you feel bad, worrying too much and stressing out, you have to be able to stop yourself from freaking out about things that aren't really happening now; you have to learn to laugh at it. And this can't be an intellectual endeavor, this has to be a physiological one.

Part of the way I deal with people and get them to start thinking is I mechanically have them make things smaller and see themselves doing it. I ask them, *"So how long do you plan to do this?"* They always tell me, *"I'm not doing it on purpose,"* and I go, *"Therein lies the problem."* They come right out and say it to me, *"I'm not doing this on purpose."* Okay, so who is? The minute they giggle at that, they go, *"Well, I just do it."* **Just** means **only**, it means you're not doing something else.

WHAT ARE YOU GOING TO DO WITH ALL YOUR SPARE TIME?

So, if you keep looking at this and feeling bad, and you spend an hour a day doing it, that's 365 hours a year, and over 10 years, that's 3,600 hours you're going to spend doing this. Does that sound like a good plan? And they go, "Well, of course not," and I go, *"Hey, wait a minute, it's your plan. Not mine."* And when you say that to people, they have to stop and consider that they are doing it on purpose; it just doesn't feel that way.

The ways they've tried to stop it haven't worked. They've tried to stop something rather than continuing it - by thinking you go further. Look at the same movie and whenever you get to the end, run it backwards. It looks silly. You put circus music with it. It seems silly. You shrink it down so it's smaller. It seems silly. You reduce it down and replace it with something you'd rather do for those 10 years.

Look at the next 10 years. If you don't look at those 58,000 waking hours as if you're going to do something with them, then you'll just keep doing what's familiar, whether it's depression, whether it's obsessive compulsive disorder, any behavior that I consider to be stupid. It's not until people look at it and they feel stupid that they'll stop doing it. They have to look at the commitment they've made to engaging with behaviors that don't work.

BEING STRATEGIC

With the Internet, with globalization, the world is in a constant state of change. Suicide rates seem to be going up. We tend to spend a lot of time going over and ruminating over the worst kinds of things and being terrified of the future. We don't only feel bad about what's happened, we feel scared of what's going to happen because we can't predict it. Helping people think more effectively isn't simply a case of understanding what to do, it's also handling the potential problems or challenges that might arise. Most people are pretty good at setting goals, but they're not very good at the next step, which is understanding what they need to do to get there and what is going to get in their way.

In the area of personal development, often people will say, *"Oh, I want to achieve this and I'm going to read The Secret, I'm going to repeat the mantra, 'I want it, I want it, I want it', and then go, 'why isn't it here?'"* That's because they didn't do anything and when they tried to do something, something that they could have predicted ahead of time cropped up and they didn't know how to handle it because they weren't being strategic.

Thinking on Purpose is also about how to be more strategic. Understanding not just where you want to go, not just where the trajectory of your life is going at present and how to move it over,

37

but also what are the potential things you need to deal with. You need to plan ahead to be disappointed and you also need to plan ahead to be scared. In order to be scared of speaking in public, you need to be planning ahead for all of these people looking at you a certain way. You need to be able to be ready for that so when you are there, you're already ready for it and you're able to overcome it.

Looking at the problem, the problem is that we don't use our brain to think on purpose. When people say to me – and this is the magic phrase – *"It's just that I thought it would be easier. It's just that I thought she would like me."* When people do that they're not really thinking. They make up an idea, they make the memory of the idea and they keep thinking that idea rather than watching what's going on. The more we spend our time doing this, the more we truly are wasting the currency of our life

THE CURRENCY OF LIVING

"In the end, it's all about time and how you spend it."
Dr Richard Bandler

The currency of living boils down to something really simple - it's all about time. Oddly enough, the beginning of this book is to tell you the end, and in the end, it's all about how you spend your time. Most people aren't even good at how they spend their money, but most people at least consider it. They'll go, *"This is too expensive."* I've brought people into a restaurant and they've looked at the menu, then looked up at me and gone, *"I can't afford to eat here."*

Either I can say, *"I'll buy you lunch,"* or we go somewhere they can afford to eat. However, when it comes to your life, people spend time without thinking. My friend Owen and I were talking yesterday; Owen told me he asked somebody how much time they spent smoking cigarettes because they said they couldn't quit. When they counted up the number of cigarettes and they counted up the number of minutes that it takes to actually smoke the cigarette, it came out to 80 minutes a day.

Well, I'd go further than that: How much time do you spend not smoking and worrying about smoking, because it will probably double it - 80 minutes becomes 160 minutes. Now when you start calculating that outright, what happens is you take 160 minutes and you multiply that by 365, and you end up with a pretty big number: 58,400 minutes!

What happens when you start doing this, you start talking about spending roughly 1,000 hours every year worrying about whether you're going to smoke, feeling bad about the fact you did smoke and you can't quit, and talking to people about it – "Gee, I wish I could quit." When you take 1,000 hours and you multiply it by 10 years, you're talking about your plan for life in the next 10 years is to spend 10,000 hours either smoking cigarettes or worrying about smoking cigarettes.

If you're 20 years old or 30 years old or 40 years old, and you're planning to live 30 years - well, now we're talking 30,000 hours, or 40 years equates to 40,000 hours. And this is just one personal problem.

Now, what if you could trade that 40,000 hours for time where you were productive, time where you made money, time where you felt good about yourself? What if it could be time where you exercised, where you improved your life, where you were making love, smiling, laughing, singing, learning to play an instrument, doing art, having music in your life, talking to your children and laughing and playing? Wouldn't that be incredible?

Everybody tells me they don't have time to exercise, but nobody says, *"I can't afford time to worry about this."* The truth is many people spend over an hour a day, most people over two, and a lot of people over three hours a day worrying about what others think about them, worrying about whether they'll be able to achieve something. They waste time looking in the mirror telling themselves they're too fat, their nose is too big, their tits are too small, the list goes on and on. They never think they're planning to do this every day for a certain amount of time.

When you start talking about spending four and five hours a day doing things that make you feel bad (in some cases even more hours than that), we're talking about hundreds of thousands of hours over the next 10, 20, and 30 years that you're going to spend feeling bad.

THE MONKEY EFFECT

Much of how we think every day is not really thinking; we have automated much of what goes on inside our mind. In the modern world, the massive amount of information available and vast arrays of choices we are expected to make have made our brain search for shortcuts. Our brain looks to conserve energy; therefore, it looks for the shortest, quickest ways to do something, and in doing so, often gets us to repeat the same stupid behaviors over and over again.

In many ways, we still act like monkeys; we automatically engage in the same things repeatedly. People spend a lot of time singing TV commercial songs inside their head and repeating the same negative thoughts over and over again. We're not even creatively negative; we tend to be quite negative about the same things in the same way. We don't worry about a variety of things usually, we focus on the same kind of worries, we blow them up bigger and make them more detailed, but pretty much it's the same stuff over and over again.

Among other things, this book is about taking the next few days and executing a plan that will allow you to get out of old automated sets of behaviors that aren't working for you. To me, it all comes down to the most important thing: *We have the ability to control what happens inside our head.*

The most important thing to realize is that you have this ability inside your head to take charge over a lot of the automatic things you do. When you realize this, you can take control and build new habits of thinking. It starts with awareness of what you are doing with your mind, how you are spending the currency of your mind, and making better mental investments. It's about thinking on purpose rather than thinking automatically.

UPDATING YOUR THINKING APPS

One way to think about your brain is that, just like an iPhone, you have apps and those apps produce results. For example, just like you know how to use your phone's apps well, you know how to use your fear app. Your fear app is supposed to get you to stay away from bad things. However, people often build a fear app for something that isn't really scary, then continue using it. Sometimes you need to download an update.

If you're afraid to ask a girl out, you need to update the app. I believe all those dating sites are there because people can't walk up and say *hello* to a stranger. While those sites supposedly connect the world together, they're actually making us more distant. When I walk up to somebody I don't know and just say hello, they look at me and the first thing out of their mouth is typically, *"What's wrong?"* because I just go, *"You looked interesting, so I thought I'd say hello."* Then, their brain runs through, *"Oh, he's trying to hustle me..."* and all these other negative thoughts. We're not engaging the people that look interesting to us and just going up and saying *hello*.

That's how I met all the smartest people in the world, I just went and met them. If your brain goes, *"Well, there's a pretty girl over there,"* and you're thinking, *"I can't go up and talk to her because she's too pretty and she'll think this or that, and what if she rejects me and blah, blah, blah, blah..."* then that's a problem.

It really boils down to a simple thing: If you're worried about what other people are thinking, you forgot that the reason you have a brain is so you would have your own thoughts, not somebody else's.

If everybody in the world thinks you're wrong, that's okay. Everybody thought Einstein was wrong; everybody thought I was wrong – but I'm not, and now they all agree with me. You go through this set of phases (even Einstein did) - first, you're a renegade, then you're eccentric, finally, you're part of the status quo. Because it shouldn't just be great thinkers that go through this, you should do this every single day.

You should test your hypothesis, so to speak. If a feeling stops you walking across the room, you should be questioning the feeling, not repeating it. If saying X in your head and making Y pictures stops you doing something you could do, then it's not working for you.

THE CURRENCY OF LIVING

Since it doesn't always feel like there is someone real there, people often find it easier to write to some woman (if it really is a woman) on the Internet and set up date after date as opposed to walking up to people in the supermarket and everywhere else on the planet, which is how it used to be done back in the ancient times.

I go into restaurants and I see people on their first date texting. I don't know if they're texting each other or other people, and the thing they don't have are the social graces to be able to look a person in the eye and tell by their tone of voice what they're really saying, and to be interested in the other person's thoughts.

If you're interested in what somebody else thinks, maybe they'd be interested in what you think; you'll never know until you just think your own thoughts. But if you're busy thinking about what other people think and running this routine through your head, all it does is chew up your currency of life. It gnaws up your time, like throwing your money into a shredder.

WASTING TIME

When you get paid, you know you made $5,000 this month, right? You go, *"Okay, this much goes to taxes, this much goes here, this much goes there, this much goes to my retirement."* You budget your money, but they don't tell you how much *time* you get. It's a big surprise for some people. You see it on the news every day, somebody's life cut short. When people find out they're going to die, they start doing things. When people turn a certain age, they suddenly throw the rules out and start acting differently, they don't care anymore.

Somebody once told me that their mother told them when they were 50 they didn't have to worry about what people thought anymore. Then on her 50th birthday, she became a totally different person; she became totally relaxed and started living. Why wait until you're 50 to do that? The truth is you should be able to plan what you want, think what you want, do you want, but you should not do it as a reaction, it shouldn't be on autopilot.

43

When your car's on cruise control, if you step on the brake or the gas, you drop out of cruise control. Why do you step on the brake or gas? Because something happens on the road. On the road of life, when you're not driving where you want to go, if you put the wrong address in the GPS, you don't just keep going to the wrong place, you go back and put a new destination in, you check to make sure you put in the right address in the first place.

If what you're doing isn't making you happy or isn't making you more productive, you're not thinking, you're remembering, and you risk wasting hundreds of thousands of hours if you live 30 years. Now if you don't live 30 years, it actually becomes a more valuable currency; if you're only going to live 10 years more, those 10,000 hours are even more important. The more you think, the more you have to go through your time and figure out what time is being wasted and what you want to put in its place. If you spend 15 minutes for 15 days doing that, just little pieces like that, it will turn your life around. When I see a client, that's really all I'm doing with them, I get them to ask the questions: *"When am I going to do this?" "What am I going to do?"* This is so that they make a plan and realize if the plan doesn't work, the plan has to change. What you're thinking has to change.

SCHEDULING THE MOST IMPORTANT MOMENTS

The question is: When you're planning, and you color-code things, what's more important on the color code? Would a meeting have the brightest color and the biggest picture, so therefore it's more important, or would sex? As much as everybody answers that question, *"sex,"* that's not really what they do. They do the exact opposite, so they never get around to it because it's not the most important thing on their list.

While it seems artificial to schedule kissing somebody goodbye and hello, it's amazing how often it's forgotten. The most important moments of your life should be a kiss. What could be more intimate? That's when time should slow down, otherwise it becomes a dot in life instead of a great moment.

In the end, all you really have are the great moments of your life. Although it'd be nice if some of those were business meetings where you really did a great thing, they really shouldn't top the list of things most important to you.

When you really ask people to tell you the most important moments of their life, you're going to hear about the birth of their children, the moment they met their wife, all those kinds of things. Yet when they think about their future, these are not the events they consider: moments with their children and other moments like these.

There are things that should be ritualized, like going to work, brushing your teeth, taking a shower, going to the gym; things we schedule in and make so whether we want to do them or not, we do. But the things that we like doing should be special and have that special quality to them. When we don't put them in our hierarchy and on the top of our life, what happens is when those moments arise, they slip by. And the more years you live, the more they slip by.

BUDGETING YOUR TIME EFFECTIVELY

If you let all those magic moments drip away, you end up with a bag full of fears and worries, you're not spending your life effectively. People even use the phrase in America, (although not every country has the same idiom) *spending time with someone.* If you really listen to people talk there's a certain wisdom, they go, *"I need to spend more time with my wife."*

The way it's phrased, they act like they're paying for something. It doesn't come out like, this is really how I want to spend my money. If you have $1,000 and you can paint the inside of your toilets or go on vacation, sometimes you have to fix the toilets because it's necessary. Most people when they budget their money, don't budget for the things that are special, they don't budget for the date nights, they don't budget either their time or their money, so they coincide with that special event.

I'm pretty much the opposite of that. I've never been late for work, I've never missed a workshop. I show up where I'm supposed to be because I plan my time well. I'm never late, which drives everybody crazy. I'm everywhere 10 minutes ahead of time because I don't want to stress on the way there. I'm not going, *"What's the last minute I can leave?"* I'm going, *"How can I get there and enjoy myself?"* I want to watch the scenery; I want to get to the airport early, sit around and people watch.

Most people are tapping their foot like the plane's going to take off sooner. They stand in line for 45 minutes waiting to get on a plane with assigned seating – that doesn't make a bit of sense to me. I don't care when I get on the plane, I care more about when I get off the plane. I want my seat as close to the door as possible so I can get out as fast as possible, because being out of the plane is better than being in the plane.

If you're thinking about the quality of your life, the currency that creates quality of life is *time*. What's also important is how fast it goes by, some *time* you want to go by faster and some you want to go by slower. Most people have that completely backwards.

The brain is designed only to make things familiar; there's nothing about familiar good, familiar bad, familiar you like it, familiar you don't like it. The brain will make anything familiar. Suffering gets familiar if people get used to it. When you ask them to try things that'll make them happy, it's uncomfortable for them because it's not familiar.

TURNING PLANNING INTO ACTION

The problem isn't that people aren't planners, it's that they don't attach thinking to *doing*. I know lots of people who have big plans and do nothing; I know lots of people who do things all the time, but they have no plan. They always argue about who's getting more done. Neither one of them is getting anything done really. One is pure energy bouncing off all the walls and if there isn't something that decides where you're going with your energy, there has to be a plan. A plan has to be adjustable.

The reason we came up with brains is they remember and know X is good and Y isn't good, eat X and don't eat Y. It was so we could survive, so that we could adapt to our environment. The organism which adapts the most to any environment, the one with the greatest flexibility, evolves and goes on. Evolution is going to depend on people getting smarter, not who's the strongest.

They may live well in a war zone with weapons or beat each other up in a ring, but in terms of actual survival, it's your ability to adapt to everything, not to one job. Jobs used to be for life, and now you can't be an expert in a computer for any length of time because they change too fast. Cellphones too. You can't be an expert on a cellphone because it won't exist in three years.

I used to be able to fix my own car. Now when I open the bonnet, I can't even tell which direction the engine is pointing in. It doesn't look anything like anything I can remember as a kid. Once upon a time, people were saying, *"Gasoline is $5 a gallon and pretty soon it's going to be $10 a gallon,"* and everybody was investing that way. Suddenly, it dropped down to a buck-69 - it suddenly got cheap. It'll probably get expensive again sometime, because like all things we conserve, it means eventually we're going to run out.

We must have people who think their way out of these problems. If energy can't be created or destroyed, there must be something we can do that would create massive amounts of energy without polluting our environment. Certainly, electric cars are a step, but I don't think they're the answer because you still have to make electricity. You have to do something smarter, and those things aren't going to come into being until people start thinking about a future beyond the way we think now. That's going to require that we start teaching it. If you're a personal consultant, a coach, you're going to have to start teaching people how to think and what the difference between thinking and remembering is.

A NEW WAY OF THINKING

In this book, we are going to answer the most important questions involved in learning to Think on Purpose: What's the difference between thinking about a fear and just thinking fearfully? How do you think about motivating yourself? How do you think in a way that leads you into action as opposed to inaction? How do you think in a way where you don't act when you shouldn't? A lot of people are doing something they shouldn't do and that has to do with planning. Most people don't make a plan and become involved in it enough to know when to stop doing certain things they shouldn't. They come to me and they go,

"Oh, I take enormous amounts of cocaine."

"Really? So, if there was some here, would you take it?"

"I would try not to, but I probably would."

"How do you know that now? There's nothing here."

It's like the fire that doesn't exist and the spider that's not there. They're already mentally paralyzed by the process of thinking about it because they're not thinking, they're understanding the way they've always understood: *If it's there, I'm going to have certain feelings and those feelings are going to make me act and I'm going to feel bad afterwards.*

They can tell you the whole litany down the road, and that's actually what their plan is. And if their plan stays that way, they will continue to behave that way; whether you put them in rehab, whether you deprive them, whether you give them electric shock treatment, won't make a difference because that's the only machine they have that plans. For them to have a *new* planning machine that makes *new* decisions, it has to do it differently.

For example, it needs to go into the future and stop going into the past. When they go into the future and they are physically connected to the future enough to feel the loss they're going to have, that they're going to lose their career, their family, not see their kids, and not get to do all the things they love to do. I have clients with enormous amounts of money, very famous public figures, and they say, *"I could lose everything,"* and I go, *"No you won't. You say that, but it's not true – you don't feel it enough."*

They have connected the feeling of *wanting* so strongly they act on it, but they haven't connected the feeling of the tragedy that's about to happen to them. It should scare the hell out of them, it should be the big spider in the room. When you do that you should see humungous pictures of your whole life falling apart around you and into the future for 20 years, coming at you like a freight train.

It should be a lot stronger than any little desire to have an endorphin rush. You should get a much bigger endorphin rush from feeling, *"I'm not going to do that!"* That should feel better. This is why I don't give people nicotine badges to quit smoking or crap like that.

If they can't beat up a cigarette with their feelings, then eventually they're going to start smoking again or drinking again or doing all the things that they get in trouble for. To me, that's not even the most important thing that comes out of this because once people realize they can beat a problem, that's just the doorway to what really counts. It means if you can do this, you can really do anything.

So, what would you really like to do? If you can get them to make better decisions about what's going to be in their future, instead of it just not being a train wreck, what's it going to be? It doesn't have to be climbing Mount Everest, it should be a whole day where more of the moments in the day are exquisite. Most people don't plan for that, so they don't get it, and if you don't get it, you have almost nothing.

BUILD NEW RITUALS OF THINKING

If you make a commitment to yourself to build new rituals of thinking, the hierarchy of the quality of how you spend your time changes so the currency of life is spent well. Some people spend their money very well; some people don't spend their money well at all; some people are horrible with money.

When you're young, often you can spend money without realizing the importance of saving. A lot of people don't have kids to help them when they're older, or their kids are not in a position to help them. When you get to old age and pensions, it can be tough. There is no country on Earth where living on a pension is a good plan. It's important to put the smallest amount of your income aside because you're planning to live a long time. The problem is, when people are 20, they're not thinking about being 80.

If they haven't done something about it, then they're going to spend 10 or 20 years in a very bad position and that's just about money. When you start talking about *time*, you're not talking about something that's going to happen in 80 years, you're talking about what's going to happen next week. If you don't budget your time and spend it wisely, you're not going to get smarter, you're not going to get happier, your life isn't going to get better, it's just going to keep looping. It won't matter which wife you're married to, it will be the same marriage. People who are fighting and having a horrible marriage sometimes have a baby to solve their problems, and I guarantee that isn't going to make it better because now there'll be three of you having a bad time instead of two. If you don't change the way you think and the way the other person thinks and how you treat each other, you'll keep having problems.

When couples come to me and they're fighting with each other and they go, *"We don't know what we should do,"* I say, *"Well, how much time do you spend fighting?"* They argue about it – which is so odd to me. They'll argue about how much time every day they spend fighting; they'll argue about whether it's more on

THE CURRENCY OF LIVING

the weekends or more this day, and then they'll say, "Well, I do call on the phone and they start arguing on the phone."

So, I go, *"I'm not asking whose fault it is, I'm just asking how much time you spend doing it as opposed to looking at each other in the eye, the way you were the first time you knew you were in love with each other. Because one was a really good experience and the other sucks. You've budgeted your time to spend all this time fighting over shit that doesn't matter in the end. If you get divorced, then torture each other for five years over splitting up your property, making lawyers rich, all because you couldn't treat each other the way you used to. You didn't budget your time well."*

I want to get people to understand, it's really that you have to stop doing *this* and start doing *that*; in order to stop engaging in behaviors of anger, you have to change the way you think. Whatever you're thinking that's making you angry, it's making you feel bad. Whether the other person did it or not is not the point; the fact that you think it and feel angry is making it worse, not better.

If it's getting worse, not better, then you're both going to do even more things to make each other angry and end up with even more things you can remember to feel bad about. It's just stacking up a block of more of what you don't want. It has to be a choice where *you* decide. Even if you split up, you won't know how to treat anybody else differently. It's not that you get a new person, it's that you get a new thought pattern.

Then, when you get a new person, or you stay with the same person, things will be better, but if you both don't think differently, you'll keep acting the way you act. If you change the way you think, it will change the way you feel, and therefore change what you can do. If you don't, it won't.

FINDING VERSUS CREATING

I had a client come in who had been pining for 10 years after a woman he'd never spoken to. I said to him, *"Why don't you just walk up and say hello instead of staring at her across a room at some place?"* He had built an ideal image of her and when he met her, she wasn't at all like the image. He came back and said, *"Well, she was a real disappointment,"* and I said, *"No, she wasn't a disappointment, the picture in your head wasn't her."*

I said, *"The only thing about finding somebody on the planet is that there's a real difference between finding things and creating things. You created a person and then expected someone else to be the person you created, and they weren't. To expect that is just plain stupid."*

That's how you tell stupid from smart. People are something you find, you find employees, you find things. Unfortunately, you don't find your relatives, you just have to put up with them. They're part of the package, one of those things in life. Some people disown relatives, and rightly so; some people are lucky and get good ones. But when it comes to friends, you know, some friends have a shelf life, they're good for three years and then they're no good anymore.

Owen and I have been friends forever. If I start being a bad friend, then he'll give me up. The same thing is true about food. Food can be fine when you're 20, and when you're 40 it's not so good for you. There are a lot of things I've had to give up as I've gotten older, there are also a lot of things I do that I didn't have to do when I was younger. That's part of adjusting, evolving your life.

HAPPINESS IS SOMETHING YOU PRACTICE

If you think about your life and the quality of your life, then you have to adjust your thinking to make it better. If your goal is to be a better person, a happier person, a more successful person, that's a good start. But if you make a picture of the person you want to be and assume that when you're that person you're going to be happy, you may be sorrowfully disappointed when you get there.

You might work, scrimp, and save your money for your whole life and you're never happy and then expect to be when you're 65. The trouble is you'll retire at 65 and you won't be happy because you won't know how it's done.

Happiness is not something that happens to you, it's an activity and you have to get good at it. You have to practice smiling; you have to practice relaxing; you have to look to master all of those things. That's why people who meditate are so much better at relaxing, they practice for at least 20 minutes a day. If you don't practice relaxing, you're not good at it. Most people practice stressing. If you're going to practice stressing every day, if you actually can predict that every day you're going to stress about the same things, especially at roughly the same time, is that smart or is that stupid?

BEING VERSUS *BECOMING* SOMEONE

There is a difference *between* wanting to be someone versus wanting to *become* someone. When you want to become someone, you actually see yourself doing the tasks necessary in order to start to live that lifestyle. Whereas a lot of times people want to project that – *"I want to be that person"* – and they have almost like a still image of themselves, which might look like that person or might temporarily be that person.

It's in starting to see yourself as the kind of person who would exercise regularly, the kind of person who would be a non-smoker, the kind of person who would wake up early in the morning, the kind of person who would work really hard or really smart that makes the difference.

Going *on a diet* or going *off* cigarettes implies you can go *off* the diet and *on* the cigarettes. Instead, thinking of yourself as becoming a healthy eater and a non-smoker enables you to start projecting yourself as that new kind of person and you'll be more likely to plan effectively to make it happen.

A BETTER KIND OF GOAL

There are two kinds of goal. One kind tells you that you have to feel bad until you get there. The other drives you to get there; it makes you crave *being*. One creates motivation and the other tells you when to be disappointed. All disappointment requires adequate planning (that's the first big quote they got from me 40 years ago).

I said it to a client in a workshop. They were telling me that they wanted to achieve something in their life and they had this picture, and when they looked at the picture they felt bad because they had not done this and not done that. I looked at them and I said, *"Well, disappointment requires adequate planning, or you wouldn't know exactly when to do it."* You shouldn't be knowing when to feel bad, you should be knowing what to do.

That's what becoming a person means. It's not about losing 60lbs, it's about *how much you're going to eat*, deciding ahead of time. Even if a restaurant brings you a mountain of food, if you try to decide how much you should have eaten it'll always be too late. However, if you literally take a knife and slice off the parts that you're going to eat and just mentally disappear the rest and eat just *that* food, every day you get a chance to learn portion control.

With every bite, you take control over it. Every time you underestimate and don't give yourself enough, or give yourself too much, you adjust that in your mind so next time you get a plate of food, you start to ask the question, *"What's the smallest amount I can eat and feel satisfied"*? When you look at a menu, instead of saying, *"What do I want to eat?"* you go, *"What can I eat that will make me the person I want to be?"* so you start to change your taste for food and how you think about it.

You're planning every time you lift that fork to not put an extra fork in your mouth; every time you lift a cigarette you don't smoke it. You'll feel withdrawal, but you'll feel good about it because you're doing what it takes to stop smoking. It only takes three weeks to get over the physical addiction, all the rest is just a habit because you attach cigarettes to all these activities. If you don't do that, just think, you get back all those hours, all the hours you spent smoking. All you have to do is to stick something else in its place.

15-DAY PLAN

N ow, what if there was a 15-day-plan where you traded your bad feelings for productive behavior? Could it be that simple? Well actually, if you consider how well you feel bad and how well you've mastered your habits, you could make it a habit and it would be easy. The trick is in knowing how the brain works.

So, what we're going to do is lay out for you a simple 15-day plan to trade your bad feelings for good ones, trade your unproductive behaviors for productive behaviors. We're not going to solve every problem in your life, but if you can solve big ones and get back 40,000 hours, 80,000 hours, 100,000 hours in the next 10 years, you can spend that time feeling good instead of feeling bad.

When you think of all the things people don't do well (and it's not that they *couldn't* do them well, it's that they *don't*), there's a real difference between who you are as a person and what you do, and most people don't realize that's only a reflection of whether you're thinking well or not.

So, here's the first big question: How do you tell smart from stupid? It's really quite easy. Most people, if you ask them, *"Are you smart?"* they'll say to you, *"I think so,"* and then you ask, *"At what?"* If you're talking to somebody who is severely overweight, and you ask them whether they're smart, they may be the world's best mathematician, they may have a memory that will win them Jeopardy, but there is one situation where they are not being smart.

If you ask them, *"Have you ever been on a diet?"* and they say to you, *"Hundreds of them,"* you can ask, *"What was the purpose of being on a diet?"* They will say, *"To lose weight."* So, I'll ask, *"If you went on a diet, how much would you want to lose? How would you know when you had dieted?"* It's all about time in the end. People will say things like, *"I want to lose 30lbs in 30 days."*

They're thinking about the weight as the purpose, not changing their lifestyle so they become someone that melts away pounds.

The secret to losing weight isn't really that sophisticated. If you're smart you know you have to eat less and exercise more – everybody hates it, but it's true. Otherwise, you'll just lose the weight and gain it back. Everybody's done that, everybody knows that's true. It almost doesn't matter, because out of the people I've met who have tried to lose weight, every one of them has done so over and over again because their thinking sets them up to fail. The following pages guide you into new ways of thinking that set you up to succeed.

DAY 1:

What are you going to trade?

SCAN FOR VIDEO RESOURCES

We want to start with an important task. What if you could trade your fears and worries for successful living? Wouldn't it be nice? The big question, to me is: Do you know the difference between thinking and remembering?

The reason on the first day we want to make a list of what's smart and what's stupid is so we can trade the stupid stuff for the smart stuff. We not only want to know what's smart and what's stupid, we want another thing that says how much time you spend doing stupid things. Even something as simple as having bad memories can be stupid. I know people who think about something bad every day, for two minutes here, three minutes there, four minutes here, and it might total up to half an hour a day.

Let's say it's 15 minutes. When you start to multiply it out, you know, that means every four days it's an hour. Even though it's only 30 seconds here, a minute there, and 30 seconds here, if it adds up to 10 minutes, well, that means every six days it's an hour. If you divide six into a year, you get approximately 60. If you divide six into 10 years, and you start doing this, this ends up being a lot of hours!

Then, if there's some other bad memory you think about and then something you worry about and something you fret about, we start talking about an enormous amount of your currency, which is living. This is your life.

As human beings, we sleep a third of our lives. Insomniacs claim they don't, but they spend the same amount of time worrying about sleeping. Whether they sleep or not, they still spend the same amount of time trying. If you spend a third of your life sleeping, just think about it, eight hours a day over a life where you live to be 70 to 90 years old, that's a lot of time that you're spending asleep. You should be good at it. I think that's important. I don't sleep eight hours a night, but I'm good at it so when I go to sleep, I go deep and wake up refreshed.

We have to watch where we are spending time. A lot of people schedule in tasks they have to do, or meetings at work, or things they have to follow through with, but very few schedule in a date with their husband or wife; very few schedule in playtime with the kids. The time they leave open for things like that, because it's not scheduled, becomes much, much smaller.

When I work with couples, I get them to schedule a date with each other. Every two weeks they bring each other out on a date and it seems weird to them at first to schedule it in. But the truth is, most of us schedule all the stuff we have to do, and that's the stuff we don't want to do so by putting it in a schedule, we have to do it.

When you start to schedule in the things you want to do as well as the things you have to do, you can do whatever you want with time as long as you schedule it in. This means now you're starting to organize your life in such a way that you're spending deliberate time and you're making sure you don't move that time for anything.

OUR MEMORIES ARE DISTORTIONS

Most people think memories are photographs of events which have occurred, which is erroneous because we process information even as it's coming in. When I was young, I lived in what I thought was a big house. Many years later I went back and when I looked at the house and the tree in the front yard, both of which I remembered as huge, the tree looked smaller than I remembered it even though it must have grown in the years since I'd left, the house looked smaller than I remembered it, and the street looked smaller. Now the truth is, I had gotten bigger, and it wasn't that I had photographed the house, the yard and the street – I had an impression, I had thoughts about them. The events and the accuracy of events, the size, even the pictures in our mind are smaller than the things we remember. They're not exact replicas.

When I ask people to recall things - which I do very often when people come in and tell me they're plagued by bad memories – I ask them the size of those memories and they tell me they're life-sized. However, they're sitting in a small room. The picture may appear big in their mind but the picture itself, very often, is actually larger than life or life-sized, but the truth is they're not in the same room where the picture occurred.

Now, when they visualize in their mind the same room where some event occurred, it's not that the event is photographed. When I ask things about distance and about size and people's faces, the answers are different. I ask the length of time that events occurred and whether the picture has an edge or a border. All of the things where you start asking about detail, there's part of it which is in focus and part which is not in focus. We're not a reporting video camera.

Even a video camera only points in one direction. It's not that we represent the world by mimicking it; we take in information, we process information, we represent information. Now, whatever we represent and however we distort what we represent may be remembered. The process of remembering is an activity. We don't always remember everything the same way; we remember based on the need for information.

When you recall an event and you're talking about one person who was there as opposed to another, the image may look entirely different. Sometimes people even recall memories and they describe themselves in it, they say they see themselves when they were aged five riding on a bicycle. The truth is when you were there you weren't looking at yourself, so it's not really a memory in the true sense of being a recording.

MEMORIES MAKE THINGS FAMILIAR

Memories don't need to be recordings, memories are working to accomplish something. They're there so we can plan. The purpose of having a brain is really quite simple, it allows us to be able to function in the world without it being new all the time. The job of a brain is to make things familiar rather than face the unknown. Most people say the strongest instinct in human beings is survival – it's not. If people can't face new situations, they'll kill themselves. People get divorced and can't imagine living without their wife and hang themselves in the closet. If they can't look into the future without knowing what's going to happen and if it feels too unfamiliar or too strange, people will take what they think is the easy way out.

The next big piece is really simple. So, to figure out the time you've been wasting, start by picking just one bad feeling. For example: *"I'm too nervous to go and talk to people. I spend two hours a day doing it and I end up with this enormous amount of time."* I teach you that you can turn the nervousness down and turn curiosity up, or something else. But how do you decide what to replace that feeling with? In other words, how do you make a decision about what you're going to feel and find a memory in your life where you felt that way, turn it up, practice feeling that way and think about doing that same thing?

In other words, that's what a real plan or decision is. You have to make a good decision because the decisions you've been making so far haven't worked. Of course, they don't feel much like decisions. In reality though, you've been deciding and planning that every time you're in this situation, you are going to feel a certain way: *"The next time I'm in this situation I'm going to be nervous."* You can predict it.

You're on monkey controls. If you're on cruise control, it doesn't feel like a decision, which means it's not. It's not really a decision if you only have one choice. It's the most important thing I learned from the therapist Virginia Satir. She said, *"If you only have one choice, it's not a choice,"* then it's autopilot. If you only have one way of doing things, then you can't decide between them; if you only know one sexual position, then you can't have variety. It's just that simple.

You can't say, *"Which of these two things am I going to choose?"* And, most of the time people will make the best choice if they have one. But, if they don't have one, they won't make a choice and they'll just go on autopilot, because if you have to choose between familiar and unfamiliar you will always take familiar.

DAY 1
TASK

List your negative behaviors and feelings

Make a list of what bad feelings you get in a typical day. Include in this the kind of negative behaviors that you engage in as a result of these feelings. For example, maybe you might worry and feel stressed and that might make you procrastinate around the house.

List the bad feelings and negative behaviors attached:

Bad feeling	Negative behaviors attached

Next, give each feeling an approximate number indicating how many times you engage in it. For example, maybe you get stressed about something six times a day or you're worry about something five times a day. Each time, how much time do you spend feeling bad? Total it out.

List the bad feelings and the total amount of time they occupy your mind per day:

Bad feeling	Amount of time per day the feeling occupies your mind

Next add it up and figure out how much time would you end up wasting in these feelings over the below periods of time. This will show you how much time you have to play with when you have stopped feeling bad:

1 week

1 month

6 months

1 year

5 years

10 years

20 years

30 years

What good feelings would work better for you instead?

Here are some examples to get you started:

HAPPY	LOVE
CONFIDENT	FULFILMENT
EXCITED	CURIOSITY
MOTIVATED	
ENTHUSIASTIC	
FUN	
JOY	

What could you be doing instead?

Some examples might be:

YOGA	KISSING
EXERCISE	WALKING IN NATURE
RELAXATION	CURIOSITY
TIME PLAYING GAMES WITH KIDS	
MEDITATING	
READING	
WRITING	

List the new behaviors you're trading the old ones in for:

This way, if you were spending two hours worrying about your health for example, you could be spending that two hours exercising and doing yoga. Thinking on Purpose means being more aware of where every second is going so you can make sure you are making the most of every one.

Now you've completed this section and reflected on what you want to trade and how much better your life will be when you have done those trades, it's time to show you how to put your mind on the controls, which is what Day 2 brings...

SCAN FOR DAY ONE WORKSHEET

DAY 2:

Putting your mind on the controls

SCAN FOR VIDEO RESOURCES

N ow on Day 2 we want you to start taking charge and put your mind on the controls. This means we want you to practice banishing bad thoughts and building good ones in their place. We want you to spend some time changing the feelings, so you can do so at will in the future. This isn't something you stop doing, it's something that will soon become a habit for you.

You can already predict that you can be terrified; you can already know ahead of time when you are going to feel most negative feelings. This gives you an advantage and allows you to take charge and make sure the feelings are changed before they take root. You're building a new program. This is where you update the software of your feeling apps.

TAKING CONTROL OF YOUR MIND

So, the whole idea is to first find out how much time you waste (which you did on Day 1), and the next thing is taking control of it. How do you take control of your mind?

Mind control is not me controlling somebody else's mind, it's me telling them where the damn switches are! Start with the easy stuff. If you're overwhelmed by something, then you make it smaller, you push it further away. If you're not overwhelmed and you should be, you need to do something else. If you see somebody you want to go meet, you should have pictures in your head that propel you forward; you shouldn't be making pictures of them spitting in your eye. If you walk up and they're an asshole, you just have to go, "I'm not going to marry them," and walk away.

I had a salesman call me and offer me $15,000 to get him so he would pick up the phone and cold call. I told him, *"It's a complete waste of money. Just go to my Persuasion Engineering seminar for three days in Florida and you'll be picking up the phone like crazy. It's a lot cheaper and you'll get all this other stuff that will tell you what to do when people answer the phone, because the trouble is you may get them to answer, but you might not know what to do once they do."*

He's an investment banker and he's got millions of dollars, but being rich doesn't make you smart. I've had tons and tons of rich clients. People think that being rich means you're smart. Some rich people are smart. Some poor people are smart. However, it's all about how you spend your time. A lot of people become really rich and they keep buying *this* and buying *that* and trying to buy people to make themselves happy. If they don't know how to be happy, they're not going to be happy - rich or poor.

It's like everything else - it's not something that happens to you, it's something you do. Being motivated is not something that happens to you, it's something you do; making good decisions doesn't happen to you, it's something you do. If it's a bad decision, you need to re-decide, you need to change the way you feel so you change how you think, so it changes what you do, otherwise you're not going to accomplish the things in life you want to. It's just that simple.

UPDATING YOUR FEAR APP

If you don't know anything about spiders, you have to generalize that they're all poisonous; if you don't know anything about snakes, you have to stay away from all snakes. Fear is what the brain makes familiar; what's unfamiliar, you stay afraid of because your senses will tell you. A snake handler knows exactly which ones are poisonous and what to do. He has the proper tools, so he is not afraid when he sees the snake. His brain knows how to cope with them.

If you don't know how to cope, your brain over-adrenalizes. This is why people don't know how to feel good when they do speeches in public – they're asking the wrong question. They're not thinking, *"How do I make the audience feel good?"* They're thinking, *"I feel bad,"* and then they're looking at their bad feeling. It's not that it's protecting them from anything - it's not protecting them at all. It's just the indication that there isn't anything making it familiar that works, therefore, it produces fear. If you don't have the programs that work, you will feel fear in almost any situation, or end up hurt or dead.

If you have a fear app and you're afraid of something, it should tell you that you don't know what to do. The fear should lead to curiosity, the thing that tells you it's time to think, but you don't wait until you're terrified. You can predict that you're going to be terrified. The whole trick is to know this is going to happen to you. If you know you're going to go into a nightclub and you're going to be afraid to walk up and say *hello* to people, then the fact you can predict it tells you that you need a new program. You don't even have to get there, it's not like it's a surprise.

People aren't surprised that they're afraid of elevators; people are not surprised that they go to work and they're depressed; people aren't surprised that they have anxiety when they get on the bus – these are not surprises. People can look into the future and know when they're going to feel bad ahead of time. That's because they haven't taken it as a message that they need to think differently.

If you can think, *"Today I'm going to be a passenger in the car with so and so, and I'm going to be nervous, and I'm going to sweat, and I'm going to be freaking out because I think he's really a cute guy or blah, blah, blah"* (the list goes on), then it's not helping, it produces a bad feeling even before you get there. Sitting in your house all alone thinking about it, you feel bad.

That should tell you it's time to think differently. That should tell you, *"I'm not thinking, I'm remembering; I'm remembering what happened, and what happened was unpleasant."* The reason it feels unpleasant is your brain is telling you to do something else. So, if you don't start thinking, you'll be right. You'll get in the car and you'll feel bad.

PLANNING TO CHANGE YOUR FEELINGS

What we're trying to get you to do is understand when you're going to feel bad and what you're going to feel bad about. Even if you just take three examples, that's a start. In the future, you may discover there are more, but when you feel bad and you know it's coming, that's what we are looking for.

For example, you know you're going to go over to your uncle's house and you know you're going to get in a fight with him because he always makes you angry, because he says shit you don't like, then you're going to say things and you're going to feel bad about saying them. The fact you can predict it all means you're on autopilot.

You could just say, *"Ah, the old codger, there he goes again,"* and laugh about it and it'd be over. But, you know, rather than changing the way you feel, you wind yourself up and feel even worse. So, you're still practicing at home how you're going to feel bad when you get there. People practice they're going to be nervous in front of an audience; people practice they're going to have an anxiety attack when they leave their house; people practice being depressed; people practice everything.

I mean, it's surprising they describe it to you in such detail, but the truth is we all know we're going to do these things. We all know exactly when we're going to feel the way we don't want to feel, in what situations and with what people.

I had a guy who told me he couldn't meet people. He's not afraid to go skiing and shoot off the side of a mountain on a pair of sticks, but he's afraid to walk across the room and say hello to a cute, young girl. He even told me, *"My palms will sweat, I'll be nervous, and I'll even slur my words."* And I say, *"Well, you know, that makes you a psychic. You've planned all this out Are you going to keep doing this?"* He says, *"I don't see any way out of it.*

Well, of course not, because as long as every time he thinks about doing it, it happens the same way. He's not even thinking of a specific person, he's thinking of anyone. I even asked him, "In your mind, when you think about meeting someone you haven't met, what do they look like?" He said, "Well I can't really see their face, just a shadow." Making a picture of a shadowy person in your mind would make anyone nervous. A dark shadowy figure that you want to date?!

I said to him, *"Okay, well, let's just do the opposite and find out what happens. Make a picture of somebody that you've never seen. Make a clear face. Make it a smiling face. Walk up, hear yourself say hello and see them smile back at you."* He looks at me and he goes, *"Okay."* And I say, *"Well, how's that?"* He goes, *"Well, that feels really good."* So, I tell him, *"Well, keep doing that and go to the bar next door and meet five people and come back."* He went next door into a bar and came back and he goes, *"That's really easy!"*

If you don't change the way you're thinking, if your thinking is producing fear, that should be what tells you it's time to go in and

73

just state the opposite; if nothing else, just randomly, the opposite has got to be better than what you're doing.

If you're making big pictures in your mind, make small ones. If you don't feel great about something but you feel kind of good about it, you need a bigger mental picture. Maybe you need to see yourself smiling more in the picture. Turn the brightness up in the image. Make it clearer. If you don't change the domain in which you're thinking, you will have problems. It's like when people tell me they can't get themselves motivated to do something, and if you ask them, they'll tell you they believe something is worthwhile, but it doesn't make them do It.

If you really believe something, it should make you do it. When people tell you this, often they've got a little picture 4" x 4" in their head telling them they should get out and do more of something, and it's not going to propel them forward. If you go to a movie theatre and the screen is the size of an iPhone, you're not going to get deeply involved in the film like you would with a huge movie screen.

In terms of learning to take more control, there are two options. It's important that you practice both. The key is you will be conditioning your brain to do it automatically so that when the negative feeling starts, it will instantly diminish and be replaced with the positive feeling. It's important to practice this every time a bad feeling comes in.

DAY 2
TASKS

Try these two simple ways of replacing bad feelings with good ones:

OPTION 1 - CHANGE THE MOVIE

Go to your list of bad feelings from Day 1.

- Take each bad feeling and examine the thought that led to that feeling. This thought will be a combination of a movie and perhaps what you are saying to yourself.
- Inside your mind, take the movie and freeze it, put a border around it, drain the color, shrink it to the size of a dollar and make it blink black and white really fast like a deck of cards being snapped quickly. Now fire it way off into the distance.

Also inside your mind, take whatever the negative inner voice is saying and imagine making it sound like Mickey Mouse or Donald Duck.

- Take the good feeling that you want to replace the bad one with and examine a thought that leads to that good feeling. Again, this thought will be a combination of a movie and perhaps what you are saying to yourself.
- Inside your mind, watch the movie and make the picture brighter and bigger and closer with more color. Make it as vivid as possible.

Again inside your mind, say the most empowering and inspiring things to yourself in a confident and effective tone of voice. For example, you could say, *"This is going to be easy. I'm going to do this brilliantly. This is going to be so much fun. How much pleasure can I stand? What else is possible? How much fun am I going to have? What can I learn?"* Notice how different the feelings are now. When you make it a habit to repeat these kinds of statements and questions to yourself you are training yourself to think on purpose.

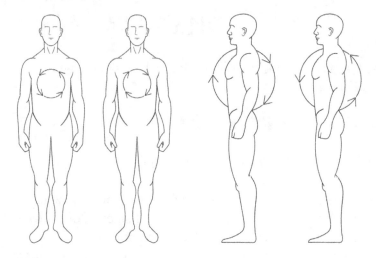

OPTION 2 - CHANGE THE FEELING

From Day 1 you have a list of bad feelings.

- Take each bad feeling and notice when you think of the negative thought that produces the feeling; where does the feeling start? Where does it move to? Which direction does it spin?
- Imagine taking this feeling out while you think of the negative thought and reverse the direction of the feeling so that it spins in the opposite direction. As you continue to do this, you'll notice you can think the bad thought but will no longer feel the bad feeling.
- Next, think of how you want to feel and create a thought that produces this positive feeling. Notice where does this feeling start? Where does it move to? Which direction does it spin? Spin the feeling faster and faster in the same direction and you will notice the feeling gets stronger.

Practice these exercises regularly so that you can start getting better at taking charge of your emotions. Many of the things you will need to do in the later days of this plan require you to have core skills that you will get from these exercises, so practice them and notice how much easier they become, and how much more positive your feelings become. Next, when you're ready, move on to Day 3, when we look at asking better questions.

DAY 3:

Ask better questions

SCAN FOR VIDEO RESOURCES

D ay 3 is where you get to learn a crucial skill in building better feelings by asking better questions. That means being able to ask the questions that set people towards the trajectory they need to be going. Asking different questions about where you want to go and what you want to achieve and who you want to become allows you to be able to take that moment, so you start to move it completely off in the direction of where your life needs to be, rather than typically doing the same thing you've done before.

Most of the time, people ask themselves rhetorical questions which review or allow them to ruminate on the same shit they've been thinking about over and over again. When they ask different questions, it takes them in a different direction, it allows them to learn something new.

This also stimulates creativity and allows them to solve problems more easily. Most of the strategies I learned over the years to solve problems revolved around questions. It's all about asking different questions that have never been asked before.

It's about asking questions with fewer or different assumptions. It's also about asking questions that challenge the assumption people have of the problem, allowing people to see there's a new way to do this, helping them see there's a more creative approach, a more creative way to achieve your goals. I think asking new questions is one of the most important things people need to start to do when they get to that point where they're facing the temptation that stops them, where they're facing challenges as they try to change their habits.

What's the difference between smart and stupid? Asking the right question. If you ask the wrong question, you get the wrong answer; you ask the right question, you get the right answer. If you ask, *"How many pounds do I want to lose?"* and you weigh yourself every day, you get to feel a little bit bad or a little bit good, rather than making a really good feeling and a really good plan.

If you started out asking yourself the question, *"How many days have I stuck to this diet?"* If you have stuck to it for six days, then you should take a day off and do another six days. Then take a day off, and do six days. That's reasonable. Instead of expecting yourself to never do something, because then you'll start slacking. You'll violate the rules one day and then the next day you'll violate the rules twice. Then you'll just forget about it.

Whereas if there's a goal it makes things easier: *"I just have to go this far and then I can do this."* If you only weigh yourself at the end of six days, no matter how many days you decide, if you've stuck to the diet and weigh yourself at the end of those days you're going to weigh less.

Now remember, you also have to exercise. Your plan can't just be you have to eat the right foods. There are a million things you could get, a million books that will tell you how to plan right. Everybody's got diets that work. You just have to pick one, stick to it for six days, cheat for a day, go six days, cheat for a day, and simultaneously increase your level of exercise. This means you need to plan.

People tell me, *"I don't have time to go to the gym,"* but you have time to worry. So you have to give up an hour of worrying and you have to make it something you do regularly. You have to pick exactly when you're going to do it, how long you're going to do it, even if it's just 30 minutes, three times a week.

If you can make a commitment to someone who holds you accountable to do it, even better. Then, if you plan these things in and make them achievable goals and keep repeating the goal, you have what you need. You have to know what to do when something lands in front of you that would tempt you.

With fear, it's the same. If you're looking across the room and tormenting yourself with overwhelming terror, hand sweating, and problems breathing because you're making pictures of the person rejecting you, that's not a good option.

That's what the guy said to me about the phone calls. He said *"I spend hours every day calling people, being rejected, so I just know I'm going to be rejected."* I said, "So you feel rejected before you even call, instead of just thinking that if your batting average is three out of 20 how quick I'm going to find the three, because if I could land it on the first three, I could take the next hour off."

Another question to ask is, *"What do I have to do to change three to 10?"* At least I'd be asking the right questions, because when you switch fear to curiosity, you open your eyes and ears and you learn a new behavior. If you're looking across the room at strangers and some of them look like they'd be interesting and some of them don't, and you walk up to three of those strangers and say *hello*, then they turn out to be total assholes, you have to back up and go, *"My picker is off. I need to look differently."*

It's like everybody I've ever worked with who's a wallflower, who sat in the corner and didn't talk to people. They would describe this to me. I've had people even say to me, *"I'm a total wallflower, I go to public places, I sit there, and I feel terrible. I'm afraid to talk to anyone and I just wish somebody would come and talk to me."* I always look at them and go, *"So, basically what you're telling me is you're an asshole."* They always look shocked and I go, *"Wait a minute, you have to understand, you know how bad it feels to have no one come and talk to you, and yet you do it to everyone. How selfish of you!"*

The minute you say that to people they go, *"I'm not a mean person, I'm just frightened."* I go, *"Ah, I'm just, there's the magic word, just."* Whenever you say it, you go, *"I'm just this, I'm just... it's just that I thought this..."* **Just** means **only**. It means, this thought is more important than everything else in the world and everybody in the world. You should be curious about who else is lonely in the room.

If, instead of thinking about how bad you felt you turned the bad feeling down and said, *"I wonder who else feels really bad? I should go cheer them up."* Then you're on the road. You'll discover how easy it all is at that point.

Instead of asking questions that magnify your bad feeling, ask questions that make your bad feeling irrelevant and make good feelings pop up. Questions are like a knife, they slice pie; this part is left, this part is gone. When you slice out the bad pie for yourself, that's just stupid. The question is, *"What's on the other side of the knife?"* When you ask the right question, you get better answers.

You ask, *"What would make me happy?"* or *"What would happen if I did?"* or *"Who feels worse than me I could go talk to and reassure?"* Instead of the things that amplify your bad feelings, good questions diminish your bad feelings and move you down the road. Then the question is, *"Which good feeling?"* and *"How good can I make it feel?"* And then the next question becomes, *"How much pleasure can you stand?"*

Once you've gotten to the point where you've sat down and calculated how much time you waste on things, then you have to ask the question, *"What do you feel bad about?"* Some might be pretty obvious: *"I feel bad because I haven't gone to the gym. I feel bad because I haven't done this. I need to this. I need to get a job."* It doesn't even matter what it is.

One way to determine a good question from a bad question is, how does it deal with conservation of time? *"What day am I going to start going to the gym?"* is a more useful question because if you spend three months worrying about it and never go, it's all spent time. If you look at time as a commodity, then it gives you a basis on which to make good decisions.

You have to ask yourself, *"Do I want to spend my time feeling bad about something that happened seven years ago?"* If every time you look at your kid you remember something bad they did seven years ago, that's not going to be very useful. Wouldn't you rather ask yourself, *"How do I want to spend that time?"*

Good questions lead to a good plan. You then need to learn to believe in it.

DAY 3
TASK

Start asking and answering the following questions consistently to help you to Think on Purpose. While doing so, think of various scenarios where these questions would be useful:

Situation:	

What do I want to be feeling in this situation?

What is the solution to this?

What should I do first to get the result I want

How can I have more fun doing this?

What do I have to feel grateful for in life?

Who makes me feel most loved?

What would make me happy?

How much pleasure can I stand?

What's worth doing?

What's the most useful thing to do?

Who can help me?

What can I learn?

What's the best that can happen?

What will it be like once I succeed?

What are the best memories I have?

What are the greatest accomplishments I've had?

Who are my favorite people?

What are the best things about planet earth?

You can also generate your own questions that help you to get into the very best state possible, consistently.

QUESTION:

QUESTION:

QUESTION:

QUESTION:

Having mastered the skill of creating and using powerful questions, it's critical to ask them regularly and consistently. As you do so, we're then interested in helping you to build more empowering beliefs.

SCAN FOR DAY THREE WORKSHEET

DAY 4:
Building better beliefs

SCAN FOR VIDEO RESOURCES

Day 4 is about building great beliefs that propel you forward. You automate behavior by making beliefs that motivate you. Some beliefs lead to new behaviors and some don't. A lot of people believe they should diet and don't - that's not the kind of belief I'm talking about. The beliefs that lead to behavior are different, and we all have them. We believe if we don't get a haircut, there's a point where it's too late. You have an idea, you look in the mirror and you go, *"I've got to go to the barber and I've got to do it now."*

> In this chapter, at the top right corner of every second page, you'll find a box that says LIMITING BELIEF. You could imagine whatever your limiting belief is to be in that box. In the corner of the box, there is another box called DESIRABLE BELIEF. You could imagine here a more resourceful belief that you'd like instead of the limiting belief. As you flick through the pages, you'll see the desirable belief getting bigger until it overtakes the listing belief. This is an example of the kind of thing that you can do inside your mind.

You have to go inside your mind and find things that get you to do something. You have to go, *"How much hair is okay and how much is too much?"* Or, *"When do I need to shave, when don't I need to shave?"* Because all of these little things lead to behaviors. *"When am I going to mow the grass; when am I not going to mow?"* Whatever it is you do and actually get done regularly is what I'm talking about. If you show up for work on time, you figure out no matter how much of a person you are that waits until the last minute, it doesn't matter. There is a feeling that goes with it – now it's time to do it.

You have to take that feeling, and then you have to go and ask, *"What do I believe strongly that I actually do?"* I mean, some people believe in religion and they go to church every Sunday; some people believe in religion and go twice a year. I'm not talking about that belief, I'm talking about the one that gets you to go regularly, it gets you to show up to things. Believing you have to be home at a certain time or your wife's going to be angry may be what gets you home, but it gets you home because you believe it.

Believing you want to go home because you love your wife and you can't wait to see her; if this gets you to go home, it's really the kind of belief we're talking about. Whatever it is you believe that gets you to do something, that's when you believe it. You have to keep that feeling moving in your body when you put that belief in your mind. The key is to notice how you represent this belief. What image comes to mind when you think of this belief? How colorful and how big is it? You know how big a strong belief has to be (including all of those things, like where it's located in your mind).

Next, consider the thought that you would like to turn into a conviction. Then, you just take a strong belief and you superimpose this one on the top with the feeling that says, *"I have to show up Monday, Wednesday and Friday."*

LIMITING BELIEF

(image of a belief that limits
you in some way)

DESIRABLE BELIEF

After this, you pretend it's Monday in your mind and find out
if the new thought pops up by itself as a strong belief. If it
doesn't, you do it again and again in your mind until you build
an automatic belief that says, *"You have to do this at this time."*
People don't think. They get up in the morning and they brush
their teeth. They don't make a big decision about it. They see the
toothbrush, they look in the mirror and they brush their teeth.
They don't take the toothbrush and shove it up their ass. They
know exactly what it's for. It's monkey behavior.

DECIDING AHEAD OF TIME

If you don't make the things you need ritualized and automatic,
and do them, it makes it harder. One of those things is deciding
what you're going to eat. I had dinner at a benefit the other
night. I got my food and I ate a certain amount of each thing. The
woman sitting next to me says to me, *"I wish I could learn portion
control like that,"* and I looked at her and I said, *"Well, you have
to decide before you eat how much you're going to eat."* She
said, *"Well, it just tasted so good I couldn't stop."* That's not
deciding ahead of time.

Obviously, she didn't decide ahead of time. She knew she wanted
to do it, but she had no plan for it. If she doesn't make a plan

that says, *"You're going to take the time to decide,"* it won't help. Even though they keep smoking cigarettes, people don't realize they're deciding to smoke. Every time they decide, it doesn't just end up in their mouth; they look for the cigarettes, they find the cigarettes, they plan, they go out and buy the cigarettes.

Being a drug addict is complicated behavior, and expensive. If you have to go out and rob a liquor store then go buy drugs, that's a lot of activity to get those drugs. That's a lot of decisions along the road. Nowhere in there is the addict saying, *"It would actually be easier to just suffer for a couple of weeks and go through withdrawal and get this over with."* The truth is, it would be.

The amount of suffering they do going through withdrawal over and over, and getting motivated to do whatever they have to do to get the money to go to the drug dealer, buy the drugs, cook the drugs, shoot the drugs; it's just a lot of shit to do to get high for a few minutes and to relieve the withdrawal. That's really why people keep doing it, it's to relieve the withdrawal. They don't actually get high after a while, they're just fighting off the withdrawal in the end.

Millions and millions and millions of people have quit smoking cigarettes. They reach the point where a doctor looks at them and goes, *"You're going to die,"* or whatever the hell it is. But if they quit and start again, the minute they start, they should do whatever they did to quit. But they're not building a belief that says they're different; they're believing they're a smoker who's not smoking, not that they're a person doing withdrawal. They're not looking at their behavior as stupid.

YOUR OLD BEHAVIOR IS STUPID

When I work with people I always ask them about them feeling bad and I go, *"So, you're planning to spend 10,000 hours feeling bad this way for the next 10 years?"* I look at them and I always go, *"Is that smart?"* And they go, *"No,"* and I go, *"What is it?"* They almost never answer because they don't want to, because as

LIMITING BELIEF

DESIRABLE BELIEF

soon as you go, *"This is stupid"* then every time you look at the behavior, if your brain goes, *"This is stupid,"* you'll stop doing it.

If you don't believe it's stupid to do this every time you do it, then you might keep it up. Everybody believes it's stupid looking backwards over a year, but they don't believe it's stupid in the moment, and that's exactly what you need to feel. *"This is too stupid, I'm not doing this."* You have to look at the line of cocaine and go, *"This is stupid, I'm never doing this again."* If you don't have that convincing belief where you can project it into the future and go, *"This is stupid, this is smart."* you will keep doing it. And that's why the first question was, *"What's stupid and what's smart?"* If you're doing something stupid and you say to yourself, not *"I'm stupid,"* but *"This is stupid, this is smart,"* then you have a choice. If you don't have a choice, you can't make one.

THE POWER OF *JUST*

People say, *"I just can't seem to diet,"* and that word **just** is so powerful, it builds in the belief. Instead of saying, *"I just don't feel like going to the gym,"* you could ask yourself, *"Is this just about this morning or is this about my whole life? So, get up."* That's how you get yourself to do things you don't want to do.

You take the same just, but you go, *"It's not just about how you feel, it's about your whole life feeling better."* It's not just about how you feel now. When you pick up the menu and you order something you really shouldn't eat, you're going, *"It's just that I'm really hungry,"* or *"It's just that I really want it,"* instead of going, *"this isn't just about this meal, this is about who I am going to be for the rest of my life."* People go, *"I love ice cream, it's just that I want to be fit."* If you take the same word, it has power in the right direction. That's how you build beliefs that carry you forward.

DAY 4
TASKS

THIS IS STUPID

It's important before you develop more useful beliefs that you condition yourself to change your feelings about the beliefs that limited you. One great way to do this is to train yourself to see your old limiting beliefs as stupid. Imagine a belief that isn't helping you or serving you. An example might be if you believed that you weren't good enough or if you weren't going to be able to learn something or do something. See an image of that belief manifested in your mind and repeat to yourself in a certain tone of voice *"This is stupid."* It's crucial that you say this with absolute conviction. By doing so, you are teaching yourself to change how you feel about the old negative thought. Notice how different it feels. When you practice this during the coming days you'll find yourself feeling differently.

BUILDING BELIEFS

Your mind tends to store similar feelings with similar qualities. To change behaviors, the first key is to associate the new behavior with a feeling of conviction. To do this, think of

LIMITING BELIEF

DESIRABLE BELIEF

something that you strongly believe. Maybe that the Sun will come up tomorrow or that breathing is a good idea. Notice where the image is, the size of it, whether or not it's color or black and white and how bright it is. We call these qualities submodalities.

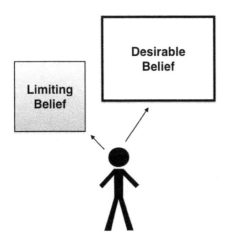

Check for:

Location of Images
Distance
Size
Color vs Black and White
Border vs Borderless

What you want to do is start thinking about the future you want in the same way as the things that you are certain about. In order to do this, you can focus on a strong belief and notice these qualities or submodalities. Then think of yourself engaging in a new, useful behavior in the future instead of the old negative one. Take this image of you doing this and overlay it onto the image of your strong belief with the same qualities or submodalities. You'll start to become convinced that you will engage in this new behavior in the future.

Repeat to yourself in a certain tone of voice as you see yourself engage in the new behavior: *"This is smart. It's just that this is going to feel so much better."*

When you build these kind of beliefs, they will help guide you to think in new ways and handle problems more effectively. Continue to work on your beliefs as the foundation of how you run your mind, and when you've done that, we will look at how you can start to build new behaviors.

DESIRABLE
BELIEF

DAY 5:
Building new behaviors

SCAN FOR VIDEO RESOURCES

When it comes to changing behavior, the question you ask is: *"What behavior do I want to make?"* You ought to make behavior by making it a belief; that's how behavior becomes automated. How do you build motivation at just the right moment? By building a belief that when you see somebody, your feelings are going to spin up, the good ones that propel you to go talk to them, to pick up the phone, to sweep the floor, to go to the gym or whatever it is.

At the right moment, it'll be there when you go lift the weight, that should be when the energy goes up. When I watch people in the gym, they work way too hard. It's that weird thing, like when you play the guitar, the only time you press the string is when you're hitting the note.

When people are learning to play the guitar, they make a chord and they hold the string down, and what happens is their fingers hurt like hell because the only time you really need to press the string down is at the moment you hit the note. If you relax, after that then you'll learn to play, otherwise you'll walk away, and you'll have dents in your fingers because you've been squeezing steel. It takes a long time before people learn to put their fingers on only when they want the note to sound.

When you play the piano, you don't just hit the key and hold it down, you hit the key for however much note there is when you're reading the music. When you have a stringed instrument, the instinct is to squeeze to learn the fingering, and that's not how you do it. When people first start learning to play guitar and their hand hurts, it's not because they're doing a new thing with their hand, it's because their hand is stressed all the time.

Their brain doesn't go for the least amount of energy for the maximum amount of result. All expertise is like that, you want to apply a feeling at the right moment. That's how you spend your currency wisely. You have the good feeling to get you to do what you want.

You should have a sense of urgency when you set up a time to go to the gym. There are things that get you to do things urgently. You know it's time when you can't wait any longer to go to the bathroom, you know the moment you should leave to go to work or you're going to be late.

You need to apply the same principles, so it automatically fires off and you go, *"Jesus! I've got to go, I've only got two minutes to get to the gym,"* whether you're meeting somebody there or not. A lot of people have such an external reference they have to pretend they're meeting someone to get themselves to show up. Or, they actually meet somebody there so they will be disappointing another person. You can just build the urgency in your mind.

You know how you feel when you don't want to disappoint your boss, or you don't want to disappoint your wife when you go to meet her at a restaurant; you know what that feeling is. You just put that feeling in the right place and spin it up. Notice where the feeling of urgency starts in your body and where it moves to and the sequence of places it goes in your body. Imagine taking the feeling and moving it through each location so that it fills your body. Then, imagine yourself engaging in the new behaviors on *Monday, Wednesday and Friday. Monday, Wednesday and Friday.* You do this while feeling this feeling of urgency in your body. It becomes automatic because you believe this is going to make you the person you want to be.

ADDICTIONS AND OBSESSIONS

Addiction is not thinking what you're doing has anything to do with the future. You think it has to do with now: *"If I take this drug, I'm going to feel better."* That's true, but it doesn't last and you're going to feel worse and you're going to have to take more to feel better, it's going to go on and on, it's going to become more dope, longer, with a worse withdrawal.

Everybody knows that, but they don't think it when they think about taking it. I mean, people lift that cigarette up because their body's going, *NICOTINE! NICOTINE! NICOTINE!* They don't think in their brain, *"The reason I'm starting to feel a craving is because I'm starting to go through withdrawal."*

They don't go, *"Hey! If I keep doing this for three weeks, I'm not going to have to smoke anymore, I'm not going to have to go through this withdrawal thing anymore, I'm not going to be craving cigarettes anymore, I'm not going to wake up in the middle of the night with a craving, then have to pump smoke in my lungs."*

They need to look at the cigarette, then look at the feeling of withdrawal and see the withdrawal as being the symptom of relief, not the drug. In other words, they have to go, *"If I snort this, I'll feel better now..."* and keep the movie going thinking *"...but then I'm going to have to snort another one and another one."*

You need to make the rest of the movie bigger and bigger, and you start looking at running out of money, your wife leaving you, losing your job, and all that stuff until it goes out into the future and this big horrible picture. Then you go, *"Okay, I'm going to have to go through withdrawal. I'm going to have to feel really nervous."*

What's worse? Losing everything you have, or spending three weeks dealing with withdrawal? Because the minute your brain releases endorphins because you feel like you're doing the right thing, you realize that's the feeling you get from the damn cigarette in the first place.

So, you look at the cigarette and you go, *"I get enough dopamine and endorphins to last me an hour and a half. I do this for three weeks and I get enough to last me the rest of my life!"* It's the same thing. With one, you look at this picture and you get the endorphins, and the other, you have to smoke the cigarette to do it.

With one, you just think, *"I'm doing exactly the right thing, I'm suffering, I keep suffering for three weeks and I'm done with this."* When you see yourself in the picture in your mind, walking through a crowd of smokers and not being bothered by it and not feeling even the slightest temptation, you want that – the desire can be stronger than the desire for the cigarette. That's what I concentrate on, making stronger feelings overcome the old ones.

When you feel bad exercising, the pain of exercising is weakness disappearing. When you go through withdrawal, the suffering is all the weakness in you disappearing, because now you're thinking about where you want to go, not thinking about where you don't want to be. You don't want to suffer withdrawal. You don't want to be thinking, *"I need the nicotine gum! I need this! I need that!"* That's not planning.

Thinking is planning. If you're thinking and you're not planning, then you're in trouble because you'll make things worse. You'll think, *"The withdrawal will be so bad that I can't stand it, I won't be able to do it and I'll be a failure,"* and you're planning to fail. You can either plan to fail or you can plan to succeed. Facts can deceive people by making them trapped in one perspective.

Smart guys like the business magnate and philanthropist Warren Buffet don't let the facts deceive them, they let the facts guide them. They notice patterns and are able to plan using the facts as information, not as limitations. That's why they do so well.

When I listen to a client, I don't have pre-existing beliefs that limit what I can do with people. By believing that every client can change easily, quickly, whether it's true or not, is a good belief to have. I listen to what will get them out of where they are and what will get them somewhere better. I'm not looking for what makes me right about some elaborate theory some dead guy made up. I couldn't care less about Sigmund Freud, yet I find Freud's work alive and well in every therapy that I've ever looked at (and I've looked at close to 300-400 different schools of psychotherapy, in different countries all over the world).

Most of them are saying the same underlying thing, which is, if you understand the problem, somehow, magically, you'll change. You'll understand what caused it. They're all going into history to find out the source of the difficulty. Well, in medicine it might make sense to find out what the initial cause of the infection was to know what antibiotic to give somebody, or to know there's a lesion in the brain in a certain place, or a tumor, so you can cut it out. However, when it comes to thinking, that's not how it works, you can't cut thoughts out.

You can't give drugs that make stupidity go away. It just doesn't work that way. Drugs do not make people smarter. They even have smart drugs that don't make you smarter. What makes you smarter is thinking further and planning so it works for you. You change the way you think and it changes the way you feel, therefore it can change what you do. In fact, it changes your neurochemistry when thoughts are strong enough that feelings about where you want to go are stronger than what you're trying to get out of. You become a force to be reckoned with.

The success that I've had over these decades working with people everybody else had failed with is because I don't argue with anybody about anything. Somebody tells me they see stuff coming out of the TV, I believe them! There's no reason not to. I'd just be careful about what comes out of the television!

I want something you can erase all the other hallucinations with, like an eraser from a Bugs Bunny cartoon. Once they start taking control of the process, then they're more apt to watch the Playboy channel than horror movies. Even at that, they're making decisions. At least they're taking control over the thought process; the more they take control of their thought processes, the more it's going to control what chemicals are in their brain.

DAY 5
TASKS

CHANGING HABITS

Think about some habit or addiction that you want to tackle, like smoking or eating too much chocolate. Imagine yourself resorting to this bad habit and then run the movie in your mind on so you see yourself feeling bad and suffering as a result of engaging in the habit. Watch as you find yourself getting worse and worse and let the horrible feeling that comes with the image spin throughout your body. Imagine the negative feeling getting stronger as you watch yourself returning to the bad habit.

Next, think about yourself changing this habit or overcoming this addiction. Imagine yourself dealing with the cravings and each craving being a reminder of how good it will feel once you've successfully overcome it. You could imagine yourself as a non-smoker or healthy eater saying no to the cravings, for example. See yourself the other side having successfully changed. Spin this good feeling throughout your body.

How does that feel? Practice it and notice how different the feelings are.

BUILDING URGENCY

Think of something that you feel urgency about. See what you see in your mind and hear what you hear. Notice where the feeling of urgency starts and where it moves and spin the feeling powerfully through your entire body. Consider whatever behavior you want to engage in and keep this feeling of urgency spinning in your mind, so you feel an urgency for engaging in this new behavior. Imagine the most incredible and desirable results of you engaging in this new behavior. Spin that exciting feeling throughout your body as well. As you do this, you will notice yourself feeling excited about the new behavior as well as feeling a sense of urgency about implementing it. Keep practicing and noticing how exciting it feels, before you move on to the next section to find out how you can make better decisions.

DAY 6:

Making good decisions

SCAN FOR VIDEO RESOURCES

M aking good decisions is again about the quality of your questions. If you ask yourself, *"Do I feel like going to the gym"*? it's the wrong question. That's not why you go, you don't go to the gym to feel good, you go to the gym to feel good for years. It's all about time and in the end, everything is about time.

It's all about time and how you spend it in order to propel yourself into a good future. If you say to yourself, *"I don't really feel like going to the gym,"* you need to then say, *"Well, that really means I need to go because I want to feel good for the rest of my life, I don't want to just feel good for five minutes."*

When somebody says, *"Do you want a piece of cake?"* and you repeat the question in your head and go, *"Do I want a piece of cake?"* the answer is *"Yes."* But, if you answer instead, *"It's just that I want to be fit for the rest of my life. I'd love to have a piece of cake, but it's just that I want to be a fit person for the rest of my life,"* then you have a way of saying no and feeling good about it. You're not being deprived, you're getting something.

It's more important to be the person you want to be than it is to have one cigarette, one piece of cake, miss one session at the gym. You make the thing you want in the long term really big and the small thing being offered to tempt you really small.

For the person who can't stop smoking too many joints or snorting too many lines of coke (whatever their bad habit is), it's only about now. Whereas if they run a long movie, it changes. If instead of going, *"Do I want this now?"* they keep the movie running and they go, *"It's just that I want my life to be long and happy and fulfilled."* Then it's different.

You look at this thing and you run it. There are 1,000 lines of coke and you end up losing your friends and your money and your house and your family. Pretty soon you have nothing. You're going through withdrawal, you're in an alley and somebody's pissing on you. Suddenly, this little thing doesn't seem as bad as the big, negative outcome.

If you run the movie, and you say *"No"* to this one, you'll be able to say *"No"* to them all. You'll be healthy and happy and all the people who offered it to you will be in th e alley with somebody pissing on them.

Whereas if you just think, *"If I do this, I'll feel good,"* that's the junkie mentality. *"If I shoot heroin I'll feel good for this little amount of time."* Then you have to spend hours recovering from it. It's not a good deal.

If you binge eat and throw up and your teeth start falling out and you have all the negative side effects of bulimia, that in the short-run means you get to eat a whole lot of food, stuff yourself and feel good, but then you have to feel guilty about it forever; all the rest of the time you're feeling bad.

Everybody you look at, you're saying to yourself, *"Do they know?"* If when you looked at the first bag of potato chips you thought, *"Is this bag of potato chips worth this big long movie of pain versus this great movie where I just become moderate in what I do and happy and make friends and enjoy myself?"* it'll feel different. You don't have to feel bad about the shit people feel bad about. It's just that simple.

Feeling bad is simply a bad habit. People spend most of their day feeling bad because it's familiar. If they would stop and think on purpose, they could change the way they feel and therefore change what they do. Change the way you think and you change the way you feel, that changes what you can do.

I hammer that home to people all the time because the very moment you need to act is just before you do something stupid. If you can get somebody to look at what they're doing and say to themselves, *"This is stupid because it's going to affect the whole rest of my life,"* that will help them. One kiss you don't make, one compliment to a person, every little bit, every little currency you spend is going to affect the whole rest of your life and guide everything from every direction.

When you keep making the wrong choices, you keep getting further off the track. Every little thing you do that pushes you on the right track moves you further and further. If you tilt an angle just a little bit, down the road you're in a whole different place. All you've got to do is make the right choice; you go to the gym five, six, seven times, and pretty soon it becomes a habit. You discover you have three days a week. But if the first few times you screw up or if you stop and then do this, then you go back this way. The whole thing is just keeping the direction.

Remember, people who aren't very good at thinking on purpose talk about outcomes, good ones talk about directions. It's the direction of somebody's life that we want to influence. It's the direction of your own life. The problem with outcomes is that often once people achieve them, they stop. We want you to continue. If you do all of these things, if you keep building better beliefs for a few minutes every day, you keep making better decisions. Practice for 15 minutes to make a habit of making better decisions.

MAKING GOOD DECISIONS LONG-TERM

You have to do the time thing. You have to go, *"It might be a good decision now, is it also a good decision in the big picture? If I'm hungry, this may make me full, but is it going to make it so I'm the kind of person I want to be?"* You don't diet for one meal, you diet over time. I diet for six days, then I take a day off and I eat whatever I want, then diet for six days. If I do that for the next 20 years, I'm going to end up being the person I want to be so long as I exercise as well.

It doesn't matter what you do, you have to double check every decision to find out if it fits. When you go to buy clothes, it may not seem like a big decision as you look at a shirt, but you have to decide whether you want it. A lot of people buy shit and they never wear it. That's about budgeting money. But if you buy something that's too small for you because you're planning to be a different shape, then every time you put it on you're going to feel fat and that's going to be counterproductive.

You have to ask yourself, *"If I do this, is it going to help the overall plan?"* If you're consciously making decisions, you need to learn to think this way. Even things like dating or going out with friends: If somebody asks you to go out, you have to make a decision whether they're a smart person to go out with. If you just quit drinking and that person drinks a lot, is this a good challenge for you? It might be a good one. It might be if you looked at it like, *"Well, if I can go out with Fred and not drink all night, I'm going to feel like I really conquered this."* So, that's actually the activity you're engaged in rather than lying to yourself and saying, *"Well, I'll go out and just drink club soda,"* and then you come home drunk that night because you didn't really think of it as the challenge it actually was.

When you make a decision, it determines what activity you're going to do. It has to be measured in the short-run/long-run as a good decision or bad decision. If it's a good decision, well then you have to get motivated to do it. That's where the thing about cranking feelings up to getting motivated comes in.

GOOD VERSUS BAD DECISIONS

Most people don't know the difference in their mind between good decisions and bad decisions. It's really not that hard to tell. They know when they're making mistakes. People always come in and tell me, *"I had no idea this was going to be so bad."* Yeah, but you knew it was going to be bad, you just didn't know how bad. It's that thing about, *"I didn't think I'd get caught."* That's one of the things people do - *"I shoplifted, but I didn't think I'd get caught."*

If you're saying to yourself, *"But it's just that I thought..."* that's the ultimate example of stupidity. Almost every time I've heard a couple argue, one or both of them says to the other one, *"But, it's just that I thought you blah, blah, blah, blah..."* [I have a picture and you didn't match it, so therefore I'm mad at you]. Expecting other people to jump inside your pictures is like the stupidest thing you could possibly do. It's not that there aren't things that you shouldn't want, but you've got to tell the person, coax them into it and make it fun to get in your picture.

That's what a football coach does - he gets to yell at everybody, but in a marriage that doesn't work so well. Plus, it's just not fun. That's why it's so important to ask the questions: "Are we having fun yet?" or "How much pleasure can you stand?" If your plan isn't fun, it won't be.

If you think on purpose and make decisions on purpose, then you start saying to yourself, *"doing the exercise is a good decision, not doing it is a bad decision."* If it's a bad decision, you spin the bad feeling up and make it worse; if it's a good decision, then you make it better.

If you can't tell your own good decisions from bad decisions (and granted a lot of people out there don't have good decision strategies) if you keep picking the wrong kind of guy, you need to have a new way of deciding. Whatever way you're picking them, you need to look at the choices you are making that aren't working for you and make them bad ones. When you look in retrospect and you go, *"That was a bad choice,"* it's always too late. You had to have known in advance. I mean, it's just that you look at him and go, *"Oh, that's a bad choice,"* you know.

For example, a decision like, *"Oh, I'll have a box of chocolates when I weigh 300lbs"* isn't a good decision. Even though it's tempting, it should be something where you look at it and go, *"Ugh! That's more trouble, trouble, trouble."* It doesn't mean you're not attracted to it, it means you know it's bad for you in the long-run. Short movies, short results. If you look at something and go, *"It has a short upside, but a terrible downside,"* then you should be able to look at the short upside and feel the pain of the downside, and not do it.

That's how you make good decisions. To me, running the short movie and the long movie, comparing them, and deciding who you want to be by asking the question, *"Is this who I want to be for the rest of my life? Which plan do I want to be in?"* is so much smarter. That's how you end up at the next thing, making plans. *"This bad. This good. Okay, I'm going to do the good one."* If you don't take time to think, you'll struggle. It doesn't take a lot of time. We're going to start talking about making plans because once you can make good decisions, then you can plan. We decide over and over, or not at all. We have to keep in mind it's about big plans or small plans. Small decisions are about big plans.

DAY 6
TASKS

GOOD DECISION VERSUS BAD DECISIONS

Think of a decision you made that you were happy with and notice the image of that good decision. Notice the size, color, brightness and distance from you. Maybe you decided to go on a certain holiday or buy a certain product that you were happy with. When you think of it, you have a feeling that it was a good decision.

Think of a decision you made that you were unhappy with and notice the image of that bad decision. Notice the size, color, brightness and distance from you. Maybe you decided to go to an event you didn't enjoy or eat food that you didn't like. When you think of it, you have a feeling that it was a bad decision.

Consider the choices available to you about your future. Which choices more resemble the good decision qualities, and which represent the bad decision qualities.

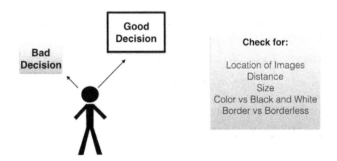

LONG-TERM DECISIONS

Consider what you are thinking of doing. Play the movie of what will happen if you take this action. See it long-term and make your decision based upon what is best for you over the long haul.

115

Play the movie of what will happen in six months, one year, three years, five years, 10 years, over your lifetime.

So, if it's changing your lifestyle so that you are walking to work for example, what will that mean over each of the time periods? How will it affect you at each stage? What are the challenges you will face and what is the impact it will have on you?

YOUR DECISION:

What will the impact of this decision be in:

SIX MONTHS

_____

_____

_____

_____

_____

ONE YEAR

_____

_____

_____

_____

THREE YEARS

_____

_____

_____

_____

_____

FIVE YEARS

_____

_____

_____

_____

_____

10 YEARS

_____

_____

_____

_____

_____

The decisions of your life will determine the trajectory of your future. Take some time to work on the exercises from this chapter as they will help you to think through your decisions on purpose, and with the next chapter, you are ready to start planning.

SCAN FOR DAY SIX WORKSHEET

DAY 7:

Time to start planning

SCAN FOR VIDEO RESOURCES

Since you have calculated how much time you've spent on feeling bad and thinking negatively, it's time to plan specifically what you are going to do instead.

This is about considering everything in your life. It means looking at everything you decide to put in your body. It's about considering everything you say and especially everything you think and don't do. This is where people really get into trouble. They look at somebody and they go, *"I want to go meet that person,"* or they look at their boss and go, *"I should ask him for a raise,"* then they never open their mouth and they never do it. Instead they make up wild fantasies of what could go wrong.

You're not going to find out what's going to happen unless you do stuff. It's one thing to roll the dice where there's danger, it's another to do so when there's not. Your brain will figure out when it's too risky to do something, but if it's always too risky, there's no risk and there's no reward. So you have to decide the risk of what you could lose. If you're spending 20 minutes a day, five days a week for 20 years, that's a lot of time. Is that time more valuable than what you're going to find out in five minutes if you walk across the room and say something?

If the only thing that stops you is a feeling, you can turn it down. Are you going to decide to control your feelings and make yourself want to do things? That's what planning is. Once you make good decisions, the next one, of course, is going to be planning. You can make a plan of what you're going to do. You can change the way you feel so that you can go do something. If there's something you want to do and you're sure it will ruin your life, you can make yourself feel bad so you won't do it. You make yourself have so much pleasure that you go do things, or so much pain that you don't.

That's Thinking on Purpose. Most people do just the opposite. They let their feelings determine what they can do so they end up doing all the shit they don't want to do and not doing the things they do want to do. This is when the mechanism of thinking is on autopilot.

Einstein said it's all about time, but that it was relative. Well, I'm saying it's relatively good or relatively bad from your own point of view, if your point of view in the universe determines how you experience it. If there are two people on two trains going side by side looking at each other and one throws a ball to another, it looks like it goes straight. If you're on top of a bridge looking down, of course it looks like it goes at an angle because both trains are moving. However, if the ball is made of fire versus if it's made of ice, it's completely different.

When you decide to pick up one of those balls, you have to be able to think ahead of time rather than just burn your hand to find out. You have to think enough ahead of time. The more experience you have in life, the better the decision should be, and that's not always true with people. A lot of people repeat the same mistakes over and over again, day by day. They worry about the same things they worried about yesterday.

The only way to deal with these things is to use your eyes, your ears, your nose, and your skin to find out. It's one thing when you turn on the stove; you know it's hot because you've been burned before. However, when it comes to stupid repetitive behaviors, since it's not a flame, even though it makes people feel bad, they do it anyway. They overeat. They waste time on things they don't need to. They forget stuff they want to get done or need to get done. They pile everything up to the end because it requires massive stress to get them started, and when the stress isn't coming from the stuff, it comes from your head.

If stress is what you need to get started, you might as well make it sooner and get it over with. At least you'll have more days where you get to feel relaxed rather than feeling un-relaxed the whole time. It's just not practical. Everybody's made really good decisions, everybody's made bad decisions. However, if you make good decisions and then plan from them, and budget your time, you'll start getting results.

Most people don't decide, even tomorrow, how much time they're going to spend feeling good; they don't put a limit on how much they're willing to feel bad, how much they're willing to talk to themselves in bad tonality, any of those things. You have to start with the short plan. Then, you have to repeat it and make it longer.

You have to make the difference between plans that go over time, and short plans. You have to decide how much time you want to be good time and how much time you want to waste. Like tomorrow, *"How much time am I going to waste talking to myself in bad tonality? How much time would I have wished I could have done something instead of planning to fucking do it?"*

If you want to become somebody that's really far away from who you are, it may require you go to college. If you want to become a doctor, you've got to make a big long-term plan. That's all there is to it. If you want to become a more physically fit person, then it's not as long as becoming a doctor. It doesn't require as big a plan, but it does require that you make a lifestyle change. If all you had to do is lose 60lbs, you could cut off your left leg and you'd be there, but that's not what you want.

MAKING LIFESTYLE CHANGES

That's why it's a stupid way to talk about it, it's the wrong question. What you have to do is to become smarter about how you spend your time. That's what a lifestyle change is. You have to spend 30 minutes, three times a week exercising. You have to spend a certain amount of time with your heart rate up, so maybe you have to take a couple of walks as well. *"30 minutes a day, three times a week in the gym, and I'm going to spend 20 minutes a day walking."*

I spend 45 minutes a day in the pool to keep my cardio up and I lift weights. That's the plan. The plan wasn't that I would suddenly get thin, the plan was if I just kept doing this and cut my portion control down, over the years I would get better. That's exactly what happened.

Nothing happened fast, but I don't have to think about it after that. A plate comes in front of me, I don't eat half the food they give me. Not even half of it. I just take a little bit of everything and I'm done. Then, a little bit later in the night, I have another smaller meal because I'm a diabetic, so I have to eat that way. However, if you shove everything in at once because it's what's on your plate, then the bigger the plate, the fatter you'll be.

At least if you do that you should buy small plates. I go in people's houses and they have plates that are the size of tables. They spread them around on there and they put massive amounts of food on the table and everybody piles all this food on their plate and gobbles it all up. Then they all push back and they go, *"God, I'm so stuffed."*

Well, if you don't make a conscious decision how much you're going to eat before you start eating, you won't know when to stop. I eye my steak and go, *"This is where the line's going to be,"* and I eat that and enjoy it. That's fine. I even plan what I'm going to do with the rest of it. I go, *"This, I'm going to eat tomorrow. I'm going to make sandwiches from it."*

So, you start by planning the kind of person you're going to become, depending on who that person is and how far away it is. If you want to become more literate, you have to buy books and read them. It's time-consuming; it costs time. People say to me all the time, *"You know so much about so many things."* Well I read a lot. I'm surrounded by books all the time so even if I sit back for a few minutes, my idea of relaxing is to pull out a book about ancient history and read it.

I read magazines about the wildest things you can imagine, everything from archaeology to science to everything because that's what I want to do. Not everybody wants to do that, but to me that's like, again, currency. You spend your time, you get the results.

You can't read one novel and become an expert in literature, which is what a lot of people try to do. They almost teach you to do that in college. They have young kids who know nothing about literature and a professor has everybody read the same book, then they're supposed to say what it means, and the professor tells them they're wrong. By the time they're out of that class, the next time they read a book, they start arguing with people about what Marx meant.

When I was at college, it was all I could do to keep from throttling people. They were reading the philosopher Schopenhauer and they knew nothing about history, about the times these things were written. It's like listening to people talk about the Bible. It drives me nuts. You have to think of the context in which this stuff was written. Then, those rules were very good rules. They didn't know that pork caused trichinosis, but they knew it made people sick. They figured that out because people kept eating pork and getting sick. So, they went, *"No pork, it's a bad meat, don't eat any pork."*

They didn't understand, they didn't have microscopes. Even some of the Jewish prayers, if you don't have any water to wash your hands, you do this thing with sand and all of this stuff and sing this song. Well, it's about cleanliness. They didn't know about germs, but they knew enough somehow or other to create a ritual that kept people alive.

"Thou shalt not create images." Well, in those days, if you drew an image on a rock in the middle of the desert, three weeks later somebody was sacrificing babies to it. They knew enough not to leave images around because of the kinds of things that happened in that day. It's not that those things don't have meaning for a modern society, it's the very fact they keep getting reinterpreted and reinterpreted that gives them meaning for a modern-day society.

GUIDES FOR YOUR BEHAVIOR

We're not wandering around the desert anymore. People bark about the truth of these things, and the truth is we all need guides for our behavior. The best ones are to make them yourself, to make guides for your behavior that work for you. That requires that you take a long view of your life, then make short decisions about what fits with it. You have to have a target. If you don't have a target, you don't know how to aim your gun. If you don't have a target in life, how can you achieve it?

If you can't visualize where you want to be in a year, in five years, in 10 years, then it's hard to move towards it. That may not even be where you end up because something better may come along, because if you only pick one target while you're on the way there, the target may run off into the woods. What do you do then? Just stand there forever and hope the same deer will come back and take the same steps? That's not how you hunt in life. What you hunt in life is by looking at what's around and adjusting.

Remember, adaptation is the key to successful living. You have to adapt to everything that happens. When you order food and when they bring the plate out, it may not be what you expect so you have to decide what you're going to eat. You may order something that was supposed to be low-cal and when they bring it out it's covered with shit you don't want. If you don't do anything about it, if you don't make a decision, you're stuck with it.

I've looked at people and said, *"I just can't eat this."* If they start to say anything I go, *"I'm allergic to this,"* so they have to take that. I've ordered a salad and they've brought it out and put 3lbs of salad dressing over it and I can't even see the lettuce. In this case, you have to make a decision that you can't eat it or you cut off the stuff you don't want. I've ordered a steak and they've put all kinds of crap on top of it, so I just take a knife and scrape it off. You decide what you're going to eat and what you're not going to eat. If you do that instead of mindlessly consuming everything that's in front of you, you're constantly making decisions as you go through; you become purposeful.

Although it's sometimes called eating consciously, nobody tells you how to do it. You have to constantly make decisions about what you're going to eat. When you look down and there are three things on your plate, you go, *"Should I have a bite of vegetables? Should I have a bite of steak? Should I have a bite of potatoes?"* If you're in the process of trying to lose weight, that should be a simple choice – don't you think? Yet people will gobble down all the potatoes and not eat the beans. They'll say, *"Well, I don't like green beans as much."* That shouldn't be the question. It shouldn't be, *"Which one do I like the most?"* The question should be, *"What fits with the big plan?"*

If you do this, you'll develop the habit, you'll start liking them. Your taste buds change every eight days, so you'll change your taste for things pretty quickly. That's one of the nice things; if you quit smoking for three or four or five weeks, the taste of cigarettes turns out bad. You have to force yourself to get to that place. When you stop drinking whiskey, after a while the first drink of whiskey doesn't taste so good. It's just one of those things. We develop different tastes all the time. The more you reinforce your awareness of making the moments of your life decisions that you are making, you begin to live consciously, you begin to think on purpose. That's the best habit. That's the habit we're recommending.

PLANNING FOR DIFFERENT PERSPECTIVES

In the national debates, when they ask a question almost no one answers it. They just have a point of view. When you see people interviewed on TV, whether they're religious leaders, political leaders, it's like they've got this tape running in their head. Literally, if you said to them, *"Is the sky blue?"* they would go, *"Abortion is a right."* So, that brings us to the idea of discussing things and finding common ground.

There is a big trick to negotiating. When I negotiated between big companies, they would come in and they would have hundreds of pages of things they believed they were fighting over. I would take those hundreds of pages and I would go through them point by point the night before and pluck out everything, then take the ideas and go one level of generalization bigger, read it all, and then say, *"Does anybody disagree with this?"* No one out of 1,000 people would raise their hand. They'd all be shocked because I'd switch a word like *necessary* to the word *desirable*, because if you change things now as opposed to slowly over time, step by step, you get to a certain place.

They always think the process of getting there is the only way, instead of realizing you can make a bigger plan that includes two things that almost seem to conflict. When we talk about political policies, this is always a problem. Just the notion of having to sign up for a political party before you vote means you have to decide whose opinions you don't want to listen to. Who do you not want to talk to in the country? Who do you not want to influence? There's ludicrous stuff.

I remember flying one time to Tahiti. I'm trying to get away from everything and I fly to the most remote freaking island I can think of. They make everybody eat breakfast together because there's no freaking hotel, it's just a bunch of bungalows. We're sitting around the tables and at the three tables next to me, there are people sitting there bitching about welfare in the United States.

They're wealthy people and they're complaining about the *"bums"* on welfare. I finally turn around and I look at one of them and I say:

"Well, you know, I really disagree with you,"

"You think welfare is a good thing?"

"Yeah. You know why?"

"Because you want to help poor people?"

"No, not really. I don't want anybody who's lazy enough to sit home waiting on me in the bank, counting my money, making my food. I'll be standing in line for the rest of my life. These people stand in line for days waiting to get the smallest check imaginable. They have no initiative. I don't want to accidentally hire one and have to go through the process of getting rid of them. It's a nice buffer in society. It does two things: it helps people that really need help, and it makes the lazy get the hell out of our way."

"I never thought about that."

That's because he doesn't talk to people unless they agree with him. It's why people create some personal insults, because they don't realize even if somebody disagrees, you should still listen to their ideas because they're not going to hurt you.

People have been killing each other over ideas. It's ludicrous that religions believe that if somebody else has a religion that disagrees with them, they should go to war, even when the main tenants of the religions are, *"Thou shalt not kill."* I mean, how crazy can that be? We're taking rules and willing to kill because we can't stand the idea that somebody has an unfamiliar belief. Especially when you consider most of these religions don't even have room for everyone to go to Heaven.

For example, for the Adventists it's pretty hard to get to Heaven and only a small percentage of them do, but yet they're still out proselytizing. It's one thing to have ideas, it's another to actually read them. Islam, with all of those rules, infidels and all that, isn't understood by that many people. In fact, Mohammed wasn't about killing all infidels, it was the people who believed in multiple gods he had an issue with. He wouldn't kill Jews and Christians because they believed in one God. What they do is they get together and they decide what something means now. They say, *"Now, Jews are our enemy!"* They indoctrinate the young in these ideas and they don't teach them how to listen, even to themselves.

DAY 7
TASKS

PLANNING TO BECOME

C reate a plan over the next year of who you are going to
become and what you are going to achieve. Be clear on the
specific kinds of behaviors you'll engage in and the specific kinds
of feelings you'll feel more of.

THIS YEAR'S PLAN

Identify the specific behavioral and lifestyle changes you will
need to make on a regular basis in order for you to achieve
these goals and become this 'you'. Plan for any challenges that
might interfere with your ability to engage in these new lifestyle
changes and plan how you will handle them.

LIFESTYLE CHANGES

_____

_____

_____

_____

_____

_____

_____

ONE-WEEK PLANNING

Create a plan over the next seven days based upon the list you
created on Day 1. Plan for all the possible situations that might
have caused you to feel the negative feelings. Decide what you
are going to do inside your head in order to change those feelings
to resourceful ones. For example, if your boss has a habit of
making you feel stressed on Friday afternoons, what can you do
next Friday in order to feel differently when he or she does what
they do? For instance, you could imagine responding intelligently
and pragmatically instead of reacting to what they say. Since
most of the bad feelings we have are predictable, get into the
habit of planning ahead of time for these feelings and prepare to
feel differently.

ONE WEEK PLAN

POSITIVE BEHAVIOR

Part of the problem some people have in changing behavior is that they fail to connect the feeling of success with the process of engaging in it. To correct this, identify any positive behaviors you want to engage in more and build motivation, attaching it to these behaviors so you feel compelled to engage in them. Here is one effective way to build motivation:

- Think about how amazing it will feel when you achieve whatever goal you set yourself.
- Notice how this feeling of motivation feels and where it starts and spin the feeling throughout your body.
- As you feel the feeling spin, keep it spinning while you think about the actual performance of the behavior and when you engage in it.
- This will help you to associate the positive feeling with the behavior you want to be motivated to engage in.
- For example, if you want to get up earlier each day, imagine how good it will feel to get more done with your day and feel better as a result of this. Spin that feeling throughout your body while you imagine waking up first thing.

HEALTH PLANNING

Decide ahead of time how much exercise you want to get. When will you exercise this week? What will you do to build motivation for every time you go? Decide what you are eating ahead of time and how much would be best for you to eat. Imagine yourself eating this much and leaving the rest, happily. When you go into the restaurant you can use your knife and fork to separate food that you are going to eat from food that you aren't going to eat before you even begin. Get into the habit of understanding the specific changes you will make and what needs to happen for it to happen.

CHANGES AND STRATEGIES

CHANGE DESIRED:

WHAT NEEDS TO HAPPEN?

_____

_____

_____

_____

_____

CHANGE DESIRED:

WHAT NEEDS TO HAPPEN?

_____

_____

_____

_____

_____

_____

CHANGE DESIRED:

WHAT NEEDS TO HAPPEN?

_____

_____

_____

_____

_____

_____

CHANGE DESIRED:

WHAT NEEDS TO HAPPEN?

_____

_____

_____

_____

_____

_____

CHANGE DESIRED:

_____

WHAT NEEDS TO HAPPEN?

_____

_____

_____

_____

_____

_____

HANDLING OTHER PEOPLE

How will other people react to my changes in behavior? What
do I need to do in order to plan for and prepare for that?
For example, if you decide to learn a new skill or gain a new
hobby, your family or friends might suggest that you won't be
any good or that you'll soon give up. Predicting these possible
responses and deciding what you will say, do, think and feel
in response will make sure that anything you decide will be
maintained regardless:

(EXAMPLE)

New Skill / Hobbie / Behaviour:

> STOP SMOKING

Possible reaction from others:

> YOU WON'T BE ABLE TO. COME ON AND JOIN US FOR A SMOKE.

Your response:

I AM IN CONTROL AND WILL NO LONGER ALLOW MYSELF TO BE A SLAVE

TO NICOTINE. IT'S NICE KNOWING THAT I'M FREE FROM THAT CRAP.

TO OTHERS: "THANKS BUT NO THANKS. I'M DONE AND I'M HAPPY

I'M DONE AND ALREADY ENJOYING THE BENEFITS".

_____

_____

New Skill / Hobbie / Behaviour:

>

Possible reaction from others:

>

Your response:

_____

_____

_____

New Skill / Hobbie / Behaviour:

$$\Big(\ \ \Big)$$

Possible reaction from others:

$$\Big(\ \ \Big)$$

Your response:

_____

_____

_____

When you plan like this, it will help you to be able to maintain the changes you make long term.

When you've done this, you're ready to move to Day 8, when we help you to understand things better and realize that understanding isn't the only thing you need to master when it comes to Thinking on Purpose.

SCAN FOR DAY SEVEN WORKSHEET

DAY 8:

Overwhelming delusions of comprehension

SCAN FOR VIDEO RESOURCES

O n Day 8, we want you to begin to understand what we call *delusions of comprehension*. This is about what we understand and believe we understand. Understanding is good, but it's overrated.

Thinking on purpose is the key to making yourself smart, to making yourself happy, to making yourself have a more successful life, to be more successful at all the things you do by optimizing the way you think. Somebody goes into training to specialize their motor skills; whether it's sport or playing piano or whatever it is, you practice, practice, practice to refine motor skills. At a certain point in time, you have to learn a whole new set of motor skills in order to be creative. You can't just do one thing over and over again and do something new.

The great ice-skaters have always made up new things which have then been named after them. Some of the greatest musicians of all time are the ones who did things totally differently. You take a guy like Jimi Hendrix, who played the guitar upside down and backwards rather than re-string it. He created a totally unique sound and played with his teeth or his toes or whatever it took to make it that his whole body was reflected in the music he made.

At the times those people do those things, there is typically a group of people doing and creating things around them. It's not something people do in a vacuum. Even if it is, it's easier if we can get more people to be smarter together. Not to just imitate each other, but to imitate the idea of doing things which haven't been done.

Look at challenge as the opportunity to become smarter; it's about looking at things that are difficult instead of figuring out what's wrong with you or categorizing it as something where you don't have talent. It's about trying to figure out how you take your assets and excel at whatever it is.

There's more than one way to skin a cat. If you're not six ft. tall, it's going to be more difficult to play basketball, but not impossible. When I was growing up, there were NBA guys who were 5'9" and they figured out how to take advantage of being short so they could bounce around underneath everybody else, jump up and make baskets.

There's always somebody who looks at all the movements in a sport, all the things that go on in art, step outside and look at what they're creating and aim at surprising themselves by doing something unique. When you look at great modern artists, or you take the great abstract artist Jackson Pollock's paintings, nobody would have ever accepted years before that you could pour paint on a canvas and develop a whole technique as powerful as painting with a brush. He poured over and over it, again and again, he learned the motor control to use infinitely complex methods nobody ever had and created great art. People began to recognize it. Then, there were lots of people doing it (maybe not as well as he did). But instead of just following, people should start to ask: *"What else aren't we doing? What else aren't we trying?"*

When we help people change we use precise questions. Other questions are also useful, such as: *"How do we optimize things? What is it we're not doing? Which direction aren't we looking?"* The whole field of psychology has done nothing but look back at the past. To me, it's the singularity of thought that, historically, we learned how to make things familiar; we learned if we do *this* then *this* should happen.

This is cause-effect thinking. Lots of good results came out of **X** causes **Y**, it produced lots of good things, but it doesn't really fit the universe. Physicists know this. The line between physics and Zen philosophy is blurred as we get into particle physics – it seems that reality isn't what we once thought that it was.

It shouldn't be just experimental physicists looking at things outside. It should be that although fire causes burns, fire also cooks, and fire also melts so you can mold things. So, fire isn't bad. If you're just over-generalizing fire is bad and you can't be around fire, you can't be around heat and you end up like my client, sitting in an apartment afraid to turn on a refrigerator, heater, or any other appliance because it might burst into flames.

That's the extreme case. So, psychiatrists call her OCD, but she's doing the same things scientists are doing. They look at this thing and they put it in a box because they're asking, *"How do we design the past?"* and not, *"Where should this person be? What aren't they doing?"*

If they're over-generalizing, how do we get them to over-generalize about not generalizing? So paradoxically, it spins itself into a new domain, so they start building the future they want. We're not doing it in school, we're not teaching kids *how* to actually spell, *how* to actually do math. We don't even get them to start to think of how you really problem-solve or how do you make up problems to solve.

I've always said there's something more important about fiction than most people realize. People who write fiction pose problems that don't exist. They then go through a thinking process with the people who read it to figure out how to solve the problem. You get a guy like the great science fiction writer Robert Heinlein - his work is powerful stuff.

Some people have simple problems and solve them with beautiful language, but when you look at these human situations and the solutions, it's a different story. Sometimes they don't find solutions and they become tragedies. To me, the interesting thing about these writers is they sit down and face blank paper. They create a whole set of problems and then a whole set of solutions. Mystery writers solve crimes. They find ways around whatever the limitations are.

Science fiction bends reality and typically becomes science in a few years. People imagined helicopters way before there was such a thing. In fact, people imagined flying machines way before that. But the fact they could imagine it means they could track backwards. You take a guy like the great inventor Nikola Tesla. He imagined that things existed. He went into the future where they existed and took apart these machines, saw what was in them and measured all the components, wrote them all down, then went back and built these machines. We should be teaching people how to do these great thought-processes.

And there are many others like this we don't know about. We should be preparing ourselves to explode into a great future rather than fighting over which psychologist knew more than others. I got a current Psychology 1A book and catalogue from a college to see what they're teaching people. It's a little bit discouraging. I was in college decades ago, and they're not doing much else now other than what they did then. They've added a few names to the list of people they study, and some of them are people I knew. The great thinker and my former colleague Gregory Bateson is now somebody being studied, rather than somebody. They used to say he was crazy, off-the-wall, wild, and Gregory was a conservative Englishman. I'm sure it's going to be a long time before they include me. I'll have to be dead first too, probably. Then they'll go, *"He had an interesting effect on psychology."*

I did, and I think the whole premise of the thing is wrong. I think studying the mind is important, but we should be studying the *good minds* and teaching the minds that aren't working to do what *they* did, to get to the point where *they* were. This is not just so good spellers can teach bad spellers how to spell, but also to help them understand what they do in their head when something works.

Now we have the technology to teach people those thought-processes simultaneously. The ability to internally remember images and internally construct images provides us with a greater insight into how people do what they do.

I'm sure Mozart couldn't remember every note in a symphony without imagining them all being written down on a piece of paper first. They said he would listen to a symphony and come home and play it. He didn't memorize it and automatically play it. There was cognition and there was planning. He was thinking about getting home and playing it again, building the machine that took him from point **A** to point **B**. How we make decisions is really important. There's a point of knowing *what you're doing and where you're going* and *how to get there.* That's where the singularity of thought comes in.

After 45 years of teaching, I believe that experiments done such as the **C** and the **O** referred to in the introduction aren't as useful as what could be done: Am I looking at the **C** or the **O** or am I looking at the problem people are having deciding which is which? Did they over-decide that all **Cs** are **Os** or did they under-decide, because they could have made all **Os** into **Cs**?

So, a person could say, *"This spider scared me. Well, I was five years old. I'm not going to be afraid now,"* then get bit by a spider because they're not careful enough. Or they could be afraid of the possibility that there might be a spider they can't see in a room, and not go in the room.

When I say *understanding is overrated*, it's because if you understand only one way and stop, you're a victim of your past. However, when you start thinking, you get a new choice. It doesn't take much to get how people create fear when you ask them to think about that spider. It's always a great big picture of a spider the size of a lobster or something, and it's always coming at them.

When they shrink it down to the size of a cellphone and blink it black and white really fast, turn it upside down, turn it backwards and little goofy things like that, suddenly they don't feel as afraid, because the feelings detach. Understanding how our neurology and our feelings become attached to thoughts is what thinking is about; it's deciding what you are and aren't going to feel strongly about. You have to be able to attach strong feelings and detach other feelings too.

FROM UNDERSTANDING TO PLANNING

The reason they call it *understand* is because that's the point you're satisfied with. That isn't the whole story. To say that you *understand* the theory of relativity is a good example. I get people all the time who go, *"I understand the theory of relativity."* I go, *"Really?"* then I start asking them questions and they know absolutely nothing about it as far as I can tell. They know one of the equations. It's like if you ask people, *"What did Albert Einstein win the Nobel Prize for?"* Every one of them will say, *"The theory of relativity."* That's not right because all they have is a few facts and they make a decision they know something.

There's a difference between knowing, understanding and being curious enough to find out all you can about something. You can be an expert (**ex** meaning has been, and ***spurt*** meaning drip under pressure...) or you can be *somebody*. Somebody who really understands will always tell you, *"That's all I found out so* *far and the more I know about it, the less I know about it."* For most people, since unfamiliar always feels bad, the drive is to understand as quickly as possible and stop thinking about it.

When you're trying to understand how a chair works, that works. If you're trying to understand how to open and close doors, that's fine. However, when you're trying to understand people and ideas and complex business exchanges, and your children growing up and changing all the time, you can't get by with, *"It's just that I thought you..."* which is what most people do. That is the magic formula to live your life in disappointment. Every time – and I want to overemphasize this – **every time you hear yourself say, *"But it's just that I thought..."* whatever comes afterwards will be your nest for growing disappointment. That's the birthplace of bad feelings.**

As soon as it comes out of your mouth you should stop and make a new picture because as soon as you make a picture that fits what's happening on the outside, you don't have to feel bad anymore. The fact somebody thinks, *"Well, it's just that I thought we were going to go to Paris this year."* I go, *"Well look, we have a free vacation to Argentina, I thought we'd go to Argentina."* They go, *"But we talked about it,"* and I go, *"Well, yeah, but the fact that you're thinking, it doesn't mean you have to feel bad, it means we can go to Paris next year or something."* It's that thing where people make this picture and they wait for it not to work and when the picture gets jarred then they get angry, they feel bad and they conflict.

I went out to dinner at a restaurant, Patricio's, and when I got there it was gone. I have to admit I was disappointed. It's just that I thought they'd be open forever. Well, guess what? I had to go, *"Well, I'm wrong,"* otherwise I'll keep going back being disappointed every time I drive by: *"Why did they do that to me? That was a good restaurant. It's just that I thought it would last."* Well your thinking it doesn't make it a fact. The minute it's not there, you're supposed to stop thinking it, you're not supposed to argue about it. People do it in relationships, they do it in political situations: *"It's just that I thought they would keep their word."* You can think it, but that don't make it true.

There has been some recent research about our neurology that suggests when we are correct about something our brain gets a burst of dopamine and so we are motivated to always try to be right, which can cause problems. When we evolved as hunters and gatherers, our decisions often needed to be accurate in order for us to survive, so our brains rewarded us with dopamine when we were correct. In the modern world, not always for survival but in life, we need to be right now too.

It's more than dopamine; we get a cocktail of neurotransmitters, and they feel really good. Happy juice, I call it. We get all the happy juice - dopamine and serotonin - when things match. When you turn a door handle and it opens, you get a small amount of dopamine. It keeps the neurology working because learning once isn't always permanent, it has to be reinforced. We're constantly re-deciding neurologically. The minute we turn that handle and the door doesn't work, we have to check to see if it's got a lock, and if we unlock the lock, then we get the dopamine. It keeps driving us to find the solution to problems. That's what it's for.

It's not just that we're deprived of something good, we actually get something bad when it doesn't work; we get good feelings and bad feelings. What happens is when people don't search, and they get to the point and they go, *"Well there's no restaurant here,"* they go, *bad feeling*. However, if their brain goes: *"I thought it was here, I thought it was going to be open."* What happens is they're not going into the what's next? They're not just going, *"What else is around here where we can eat?"* Or do what I did and go home and see if Patricio's have another restaurant somewhere.

If you go and look for the next thing rather than hold on to the picture, you are in much better shape. If you think *"I thought you were going to love me forever,"* you have a picture in your head. Purposeful thinking is to know when the picture doesn't work anymore and not stay in the bad feeling. You're not supposed to keep the bad representation. A model is only as valuable as when it works.

The Periodic Chart of the chemical elements does some things and not others, but it's not true – remember? We know there's no neutron, however we still built millions of things out of it, so it's a valuable model. Models are not designed to be true or false - they're guides for your behavior. When a model ceases to be a useful guide, you have to make a new decision. The minute you feel bad - what's making you feel bad? The outside world or the picture? If you make a good decision, you can be gone from a bad situation.

If your husband is treating you badly, all you have to do is decide to be somewhere else. I didn't say it would be easy, but it amazes me that people stay in horrible neighborhoods and tell me they can't move. I know, I came from one. But I figured out there were people dropping dead around me and I said, *"I've gotta get the fuck out of here. I don't care how hard it is or what hovel I live in."* I actually went and lived in a worse place because where I lived in the ghetto, I had a giant apartment for 90 bucks a month. I ended up living in an ft. x ft. trailer that leaked in somebody's backyard. However, it was a nice backyard and it was in a neighborhood where I flourished.

It's like, if you have a long enough plan, instead of thinking, *"Well, I have to move from this ghetto house to one that's just like it in a suburb, and those rents are 10 times what these are, so I could never do it,"* you don't have to look at the long-range plan. If kids are dropping dead on the streets, you got to get your kids over to Kansas on a farm community and get a job picking corn if that's what it takes. However, it's so familiar to be in that neighborhood so people stick with what they know, even if it's full of dangerous people.

I understand why refugees want to get out of war zones, but with the directions they go in, they always run where all the other refugees are running. That's probably the wrong direction because it's going to be crowded. It's just not very good thinking. They're just reacting. If you look at millions of them, they could overrun 60,000 warriors. I mean you've got 6,000,000 refugees and 60,000 fighters. There's just no planning in all of this. War is messy, but as individuals they don't really think of the situation and where they are.

With all the things we do in life, you have to make decisions, you have to make decisions about your life. If you decide what rock you're going to hide behind rather than how you're going to change your life so you'll never be in bad situations, that's one thing. However, if you decide that how you're going to end up in a good situation is by just running off to nowhere, it's not really much of a plan.

I know when somebody's shooting at you it's a good plan, but by the same token, it's not like any of this should have been a surprise to people. The Middle East is a mess. I really feel sorry for all those people, I do. It's probably not going to get cleaned up in our lifetime. Who knows? I didn't ever think the Berlin Wall would come down either. It's funny what time will take care of. It really just requires some people do the right things. There is no Berlin Wall, in fact, they broke it. It was the funniest thing. It was the symbol of communism and they ended up breaking it into little pieces and selling the bits.

DAY 8
TASKS

Consider any problem or limitation you perceive that you have. Examples might include:

I can't flirt successfully with a girl that I like.

I'll never be able to stay on that diet.

This relationship can't get better. I'm stuck in it.

I'll never make friends in a new city.

I could never become a successful entrepreneur.

I can't handle my stressful job.

Your Limitations:

_____

_____

_____

Ask yourself:

Have I ever been wrong?

_____

_____

_____

What else is possible?

_____

_____

What is another way of doing this?

_____

_____

What do I want to achieve?

_____

_____

What stops me?

_____

_____

What would happen if I could?

_____

_____

_____

_____

Consider anything that you do and do well. Examples might include:

Helping other people with advice

Remembering people's names

Working out

Being disciplined at work

Organizing the household

Your Skills

_____

_____

_____

Ask yourself:

How can I improve this exponentially?

_____

_____

What else can I do to get better?

_____

_____

_____

What would be possible if I did my absolute best?

_____

_____

_____

PLANNING TO AVOID DISAPPOINTMENT

When looking forward to the future, see yourself handling the various possibilities that may arise, all in the most useful state possible. Consider anything that leads to disappointment. Write a list of your expectations of things that you expect will and won't happen. Figure out exactly what would make you feel disappointed. Next go through each item and decide what do you want to feel instead. Imagine whatever item it was happening/ or not happening and imagine feeling that new feeling instead of disappointment. Ask yourself:

> "What do I need to do to change how I feel given the difference between my expectations and reality?"

For example, if you are going on vacation to New York and you want to see the Empire State Building, imagine yourself going to New York and NOT seeing it but still having an amazing time. Train yourself to be okay regardless of what does or doesn't happen.

POTENTIAL DISAPPOINTMENT:

DESIRED FEELING:

STRATEGY TO GET YOU THERE:

_____

_____

_____

_____

_____

POTENTIAL DISAPPOINTMENT:

DESIRED FEELING:

STRATEGY TO GET YOU THERE:

_____

_____

_____

_____

_____

_____

POTENTIAL DISAPPOINTMENT:

> ( )

DESIRED FEELING:

> ( )

STRATEGY TO GET YOU THERE:

_____

_____

_____

_____

_____

_____

As you complete exercises such as these, you are really starting to build smart ways to tackle challenges you face on a regular basis. Something else that is important and will be covered next is how to become more relaxed in your life.

SCAN FOR DAY EIGHT WORKSHEET

DAY 9:

Becoming relaxed

SCAN FOR VIDEO RESOURCES

The key is to start by being relaxed, then being confident. You can't confuse the two because you don't just take your stress and turn it into confidence. We have to teach people how to take their feelings, speed them up and get more stressed out, then slow them down and spin them in the opposite direction to become more relaxed.

Then we get to the big question: What should you feel? If you're making a picture of your wife screwing some other guy, you're going to be stressed out. If you make a picture of her doing it with you, you'll probably feel better. That's simple logic. Whether she is or not, that's still going to be a better picture.

There's a difference between whether something's happening and whether you're worrying about it. Worrying about it is only going to make it more likely to happen. If you come home and you're all pissed off for no reason, eventually she will. If she is and you come home and you're a lot nicer than he is, then she'll probably stop. It's one of those self-fulfilling prophecies. It's like going up to somebody and going, *"Do you like me? Do you like me? Do you like me?"* Eventually they're going to want to kill you.

I stayed in this hotel once and when I went downstairs they had speed-dating going on. I swear to God, it was the best comedy show I'd seen in years. These people would sit down at the table and they were all so tense, they would come out with this jabbering shit about themselves. Their teeth were gritted, some of them couldn't speak, their eyes were popping out of their heads.

If any of them had just taken a deep breath and relaxed and spun the feelings inside, like we did on Day 2, they could have just looked at the person and made a far better impression. How much can you say in five minutes? It was like a chess game - *move, move, move!* It was ridiculous. Even in that situation nobody put down their telephone. Even if they didn't fuss with it, they held it. Phones have become like pacifiers now. What's funny is, mine rings and I don't answer it because I've got an answering machine. In fact, I turn the bell off, so it mostly just vibrates.

People get upset. They look at me, *"Do you need to answer that?"* I go, *"No, do you?"* I actually don't get that many calls in a day. I realize if I was trying to run a business I would get more, but for many people it's like it's more comfortable to hold their phone because it's not comfortable in their mind.

That's what it tells me. As soon as somebody is clutching their phone, I know they're in their head spinning a million miles an hour. They don't know how to slow down the pictures; they don't know how to slow down the voice; they don't know how to lower the voice; they don't know how to make the inflection of their voice go down at the end of a sentence. Everything has got an upward inflection these days; even if it isn't a question, it's a question.

We need to show them how your inflection goes up and down, and go, *up, down, up, down,* so that they can say relax and comfortable in a relaxing way. They need to learn to make pictures of comfortable things, getting good feelings inside themselves. They need to relax. Then, they need to ask themselves the question,

"What do you worry too much about?" They need to make the pictures of that thing and saturate them with relaxing feelings.

When you do this, the next step is to make a plan about what you're going to do about it, when you're going to do it, and then forget about it until then. You have to use a time-loading strategy for these people. For example, have them think, *"This is a real problem. I'm going to worry about it on Tuesday when I'm with the person and talk about it."* Then, you help them to just forget about it until then and have it pop up when they're in the situation. Going through it all week in their mind isn't going to help.

Most of these people can't relax at all. But once you can, you will be able to think better. The purpose of relaxing is so you can clear your mind, make decisions about what you really want to do or really want to try. Before you go do it, you will know how to go into the appropriate state; the state we recommend most of the time is confidence.

PLANNING TO CONQUER STRESS

Whenever things are unfamiliar, the only thing familiar is distress about them. People have voices flying at a million miles an hour in their head. The insomniac can't sleep; he stresses about relaxing, which is the ultimately irony itself. The faster you talk, the less you can get to sleep. You always think, *"I'll never get up, I'll never get up."* People stress about being on time. People stress in all these situations and they know they're going to do it ahead of time; they can tell you what they're going to stress about tomorrow. It's predictable.

For four decades now, I've been asking people, *"What do you want?"* and they go, *"I want you to hypnotize me, so I can be more relaxed."* When I look back at them, I never say *"Yes"* or *"No,"* I always go:

"When?"

"Today."

"So, you just want to be relaxed today? That's not a problem."

"No, no, I need to be relaxed."

"When?"

"More of the time."

"Which time?"

"Well, when I get stressed."

"You want to relax when you get stressed? That sounds like a conflict to me."

It's because they're not asking the right questions that they have a problem. They're not going, *"Where would I normally be stressed?"* They can't even imagine not being stressed at that moment. They go, *"Well, when I talk to my boss, or when I'm at work I worry about what my wife is doing."* Whatever it is, they'll give me a list.

We need a list of *when are you going to feel stress*. If you ask somebody to think about it now, they'll stress about it now even though they're not in the situation. This means the stress doesn't come from the situation, the stress comes from how they think about it. By this time, we should have taught them how to spin feelings as described on Day 2.

DAY 9
TASKS

PLANNING TO AVOID STRESS

- Make a list of situations or thoughts that normally produce stress for you.
- Go through each one.
- Notice the images attached and the way you are talking to yourself. Notice what you are saying.
- As you think about it, notice the feeling of stress and how it moves through your body.
- Imagine taking the feeling out and spin it in the opposite direction.
- Change the tone of your inner voice and make it slower and more laid back.
- Take any images of your worries and shrink them and white them out.
- Think of yourself as being relaxed and comfortable.
- Imagine spinning relaxation throughout your body as you think these thoughts.

PLANNING FOR MORE COMFORT

- Make a list of situations in which you want to be relaxed. Imagine yourself in each situation handling whatever it is while spinning relaxation throughout your body.
- Go to the places where you normally feel stressed just with the sole purpose to practice feeling relaxed there. For example, if you typically find yourself stressed in a particular office or boardroom, take time to go there.
- Sit there and spin relaxing feelings throughout your body as you do so.

You are literally training yourself to be relaxed in that situation. Exercises like these ensure that you are building a habit of long-term relaxation so that you can feel comfort when you most need to. Next, we will explore confidence and how you can build feelings of confidence into your life.

DAY 10:

Becoming confident

SCAN FOR VIDEO RESOURCES

C onfidence is not just a state of mind; confidence is like happiness. These are modifiers, they modify a state. You can be confident you're depressed, or you can be confident you're happy. You can be confident you're the right person for a job or you can be confident no one will ever hire you. So, you want to master confidence and aim it. It's like a cannon.

This is the difference between putting a penny in your life gun and putting in a silver dollar. When you turn around and aim confidence, you will blow something over. That's when opportunity doors open, that's when you get results.

Confidence comes with relaxing. When you do a job interview, the people who say to you, *"Hey, you're so relaxed and confident,"* do so because you know how to control your state. If you're confident and nervous, it doesn't work – *"I'm ab-b-sol-utely s-sure I'm the r-r-right person for this job."* That just doesn't sound right. It's got to have a downward inflection in your voice with your eyebrows down. You can't be fazed by the stuff that people throw at you, no matter what it is.

It's also important how you speak to yourself. If your internal voice sounds doubtful, tentative, or stutters, then that's not going to help you feel how you want. If it doesn't sound loud and strong and confident and assertive, then the first thing you need to do is adjust your internal dialogue.

A lot of people want to learn how to speak a language the way you would if you were born in that country, yet internally, they say the foreign language with an English accent. I had a person who was originally from Belgium and when he spoke English, he had a thick Belgian accent. He said, *"I want to sound more like an American,"* and I asked, *"What kind of American? Do you want to sound like you're from New York? Do you want to sound like you're from Texas? Do you want to sound like you're from California?"* He said, *"What difference does it make?"* and I said, *"It makes all the difference in the world because if you're going to confidently sound like an American, you have to have an internal dialogue that sounds like that."*

If you're learning a language, you've got to match your internal state with your external state. So, if you want a real New York accent, you could say something like a New Yorker inside your head and listen to how you talk on the outside and match it.

If you want to sound confident and you have an internal voice that's all doubtful and uncertain and stuttering, it's going to be really hard to put on a strong voice on the outside. You not only want to feel confident and spin good feelings, you want to sound confident on the inside. It's important to be saying confident things like, *"This is a piece of cake,"* even if you're not sure of it yet. When you give a speech or when you talk to your friend or when you ask for a date, you should have the most certainty in your voice that will get you the response you want.

You don't want to go up and demand somebody go out with you because they might think, *"What an ass, I don't want to."* It's good to adjust that internal voice until you find the one that will work. If you go up and you're scared when you ask for a date, you'll make the other person uncomfortable. You have to imagine your voice becomes the other person's feelings. If you're going to talk to this group or talk to this person or talk to your child or talk to your wife, you need your voice to create the feeling you want inside of them. That's what real confidence is.

When I go in a restaurant, I don't demand good service because if I do, I'll probably get spit in my food. I want that waiter to come to the table as often as possible, so I try and make them feel really good while they're there. It's not that I have to confidently decide what I want. I will even ask them what they think is good. Most of the time I'm not going to pick what they suggest, I want them to be thinking about what feels good so that they do.

I smile at them and I make jokes with them. Even when it's crowded and it's busy, I go, *"You seem swamped tonight, you poor thing."* They'll say to me, *"Oh God yeah, I'm really busy."* So I say, *"Well, when you get time, can you bring me this?"* They'll almost always bring it right back because you don't get lost in the crowd, you make them feel special. To me, everybody's always worried about how they feel, and I think you should worry about what other people feel. That's what real confidence is.

It's the knowledge you don't have to worry about how you feel because if you make the people on the outside feel good, you'll feel fine. All you have to do is adjust your internal dialogue and adjust your feelings so you have concern for other people, so you're cheerful, so you make people smile and you have a sense of humor.

If you're always thinking, *"Well, I don't feel good enough. I can't just walk up to this girl and say hello; I can't make this sales call; I can't go and talk to my boss; I could never talk to my children about this,"* that's not helpful. If you're too worried about yourself, you won't be concerned about the other people.

Somebody asked me had I talked to my daughter about when she was going to start dating, and I said, *"Yeah, I taught my daughter to not do anything she doesn't feel she wants to. It's important to be able to say no."*

They asked, *"Well, how can you be certain you got it across to her?"* I said, *"She tells me no all the time. So, when she's stubborn with me, I know she could be stubborn with anybody."* One of her teachers called me on the phone once and said my daughter was being stubborn. I said, *"Yes..."* and waited, and they went, *"At school, your daughter should do what I tell her to."* I said, *"So, what you're telling me is my daughter should do what any older man says. Is that what you're saying?"* As soon as I said that, he said, *"Oh I don't mean that; I don't mean that!"* However, the fact that she could be strong in herself, that's what's important. Everybody's got to get that.

You have to understand your own feelings are not something you can't adjust. If you make big pictures of things going wrong, then you're going to feel bad. However, if you keep your mind on what the plan is, such as, *"I want to end up with this person doing this or liking me or saying yes,"* it doesn't mean you'll get it, but you have to understand if this person doesn't, somebody else will.

If you go for something, you can't be worried about your own feelings, you have to adjust them so you want to know what answer you get. So, if you get a no, you go somewhere else until you get a yes. If a waiter comes up and is unpleasant to me in a restaurant, I ask for another one. I just go up to the manager and say, *"I want a different waiter."* When they ask, *"Why do you want a different waiter?"* I say, *"I don't like them. I want a different waiter. I don't want them to wait on me, I want that one to wait on me."* They smile and give you a different waiter.

When you go up to somebody and you ask them for a date, if they treat you badly, be glad you didn't marry them. Having confidence is when if you feel right and you sound right and don't get the right response, then you move on and avoid wasting your time. You make the sales call and you start talking to somebody, if they're a total jerk and you have self-doubt, you'll stay on the phone, or you'll hang up and feel bad about it.

However, the smartest approach is to go inside yourself and make yourself feel good; go to the best time you can remember, wherever the most confidence is, spin the feeling inside of you, and make sure your internal dialogue has a certain sound to it. Then, you learn to match that on the outside. This is what we do.

Our behavior matches our internal representations. If you feel fear, you'll sound fearful, but if you feel fear and you sound terrified inside your head, you're not going to be able to exude confidence because it won't be there.

Everybody knows when you're pretending. When people say they can't overcome their fears, that's just bullshit, they just don't know what to do. When you change the way you think, you'll see the outcome you want. You'll see yourself doing the right things and you'll see it working and you'll say to yourself, *"This is going to work!"* Then, the key is to just go do it that way and listen to your voice so it sounds confident. Then, you get the right response.

Confidence is something that you do, it's not something that happens to you. You don't suddenly become confident and then you're always confident. Sometimes you'll feel confident and then in certain situations you'll feel awkward. When you feel awkward, you need to pull back and redo yourself.

During a training I've brought people up on the stage and they say something unexpected. I think to myself, *"Well, this is awkward."* However, instead of blowing it, I adjust myself, then I adjust them.

When you feel awkward, it just means you have no plan; when you feel doubtful, it just means you're playing too much attention to you and not what you want to accomplish.

Bad feelings are supposed to tell you to stop. Being scared is supposed to tell you to avoid something, not everything. Being frightened doesn't mean you avoid the situation, it means you become cautious. Good caution means you make a better plan to find out how to safely do what you want to do. It's amazing how many things in this life are not life and death, yet people act like they are.

Making a cold call to a business, walking up to somebody in a room who seems interesting and talking to them; these things should not be life or death. No one's going to die. I know people who are afraid to go up to a loan officer in a bank and ask for a loan. When you really think about it, the worst that can happen is they'll feel something's wrong with you and say *no*. However, if you put your best foot forward, you'll have a chance to get good results.

So, how do you put your best foot forward? You put on the right feelings and you put the right sounds in your head, therefore it'll come out of your mouth that way, out of your movement that way, out of your gestures that way, not a still picture, but a movie you can step inside of that tells you how to adjust. You need to listen to yourself talk so you can observe how you are doing it and notice what you're feeling so you stay in the right state.

You can influence other people around you. The purpose of being confident should be looked at. You want to be confident enough to do what? Just because you're confident doesn't mean you know something will work, it means you'll do your best to get it to work. There's a real difference between those two. You have a plan and the plan starts failing, you start adjusting the plan; you don't start being disappointed and stop.

For example, somebody looks across the room and sees a beautiful woman. She looks at him and then she looks back and pushes her hair away. People think she's distracted, but we don't know that, we're not mind readers. If you want somebody to pay attention to you, you get their attention. I can't tell you how many times I've told single guys who've told me they're afraid to walk across the room to meet somebody to just look at them and take their finger and gesture towards themselves.

Make them walk across the room if you're too scared. After you do that a couple of times, you going across the room becomes easier as you realize it's not that big a deal. The big deal is you have huge pictures in your head, rather than smaller ones that are plans. The only big pictures in your head should be ones that make you feel great, all the rest of them should be pretty small and adjustable.

DAY 10
TASKS

CONFIDENCE BOOSTER

- Think of a time when you felt really confident.
- Notice where the feeling starts in your body and move that feeling throughout your body.
- Spin it faster and faster and notice how the feeling intensifies.
- Imagine it all over you and see yourself doing whatever you want to do feeling this way, powerfully. For example, you could imagine yourself talking to that person that you like or speaking to an audience while feeling this feeling.
- As you practice this, you will start to find yourself associating the feeling of confidence with these situations and you will start to feel it every time you think of them.

CONFIDENCE TALKER

Tell yourself exactly what you want to achieve and do so in a confident and strong inner voice. Make sure that you start communicating useful and resourceful ideas to yourself with a sense of certainty. Some examples that might work well are:

I am going to nail this interview.

She is going to say Yes.

Nothing can stop me.

I am going to win.

I'm a champion.

They're lucky to know me.

This is going to be easy.

I am so smart.

I can do this.

Everybody will love it.

Or you can create your own:

CONFIDENT MANTRAS

CONFIDENT TO ADAPT

- Imagine yourself doing what you want to do with enormous confidence.
- Imagine yourself doing it and not getting the results. See yourself changing what you are doing and getting better results. For example, imagine yourself being rejected from selling something or requesting something. Imagine how you respond in this context.
- See yourself adjusting and learning from the situation accordingly. Think of yourself as a learning machine. No matter how often you hear no or fail, you learn from the feedback and move forward, certain you will succeed.

Keep doing this regularly and build a sense of confidence into all that you do. The more you do it, the more you will find yourself handling your life with confidence and self-belief, and next we will look at how you can boost your motivation powerfully in Day 11.

SCAN FOR DAY TEN WORKSHEET

DAY 11:
Building motivation

I believe there are two types of motivation. You have to wind yourself up to do something big, which is going into the confident relaxed state and the go-forward state. Then there's the one that's all about perseverance and discipline.

The big picture goes like this. Most people look into the future and go, *"I'd be happy if I was 40lbs lighter, if I made twice as much money, if I built a room on my house, if I cleaned my garage,"* etc. It almost doesn't matter what it is, that's not really a plan. They don't build a thing by which they can see themselves enjoying the process of getting where they want to go. *"I'd like to find a better job, then I'll be happy."*

There used to an old TV commercial where somebody took a trip around a cruise liner and they said, *"Getting there is half the fun!"* Well, getting there should be most of the fun. Most people are moving away from what they don't want. They slice off a part of their life and go, *"This is bad."* Then they wait until the last minute to do things because it's more unpleasant than planning ahead.

It's a New Year and you decide to start going to the gym. It's amazing how many people sign up for six months and go once or twice, then six months later they're feeling guilty about having not gone. The plan doesn't include the details it needs to actually get there; you're not setting it at a time where you can actually leave early enough to get there.

An hour before it's time to go the gym, I change into my clothes and I put my keys and my hat and my gloves by the door. As it approaches, I know how long it'll take to drive there so I don't feel stressed about going. Everything is conveniently laid out so whenever I get to the gym, the time is set aside and I enjoy being there as opposed to figuring out how to overcome difficulty. People need to make a plan to motivate themselves to enjoy.

If you wake up in the morning and you plan your morning by going, *"If I get dressed really fast, I can sleep for five more minutes."* Or *"If I take this shortcut, I can drive for 10 fewer minutes."* It's all based on nothing going wrong and it all working out. Even that snooze button on the alarm clock that lets you sleep for 10 more minutes was built by modeling people who have bad motivation strategies. It's not that they're bad in and of themselves, it's just that they're unpleasant; you have to build up lots of stress to prepare yourself to do something.

People tell me they want to write a book. That's a lot different from saying they're going to write a book. When you ask people, *"What's going to be on the first page?"* they go, *"Well, I've tried to write the introduction."* You can't actually introduce something until you know what it is. That's like being introduced to somebody and you didn't know who it was! *"We have a guest star on tonight! Introduce him!"* And you ask, *"Who is he?"* and they go, *"We're not telling you."*

You have to decide what you want to say. They teach you in literature class to make outlines; I don't do that. I just know I have to start here and I want to get there, and I have to break it down into pieces in-between. It may fall into chapters and it may fall into parts, it doesn't really matter what it falls into, but as I complete each of those pieces, the closer I get to being finished and the better it feels.

I interviewed a World Record-breaking athlete once. When he was in college and started running, he didn't really practice that much. He stayed up too late and partied too much and he came in second in a race. His response, *"Imagine how well I could do if I really applied myself."*

This you don't hear from people. When people come to me, they tell me what they haven't done or how hard it is or how many time they've failed. They're cataloging all the things that won't help; they're not asking the questions that propel them into the future with enthusiasm. It reminds me of if you blew up a balloon and let out the air - the further along you get, the less stress you have.

It should be just the opposite: the closer you get to the end, the more passion you should have. It should be more exciting the closer you get to finishing something. The other thing is a lot of people, if they know where they're going, feel as if they've done it. If you feel as if you've done something and that makes it so you don't want to do it – excuse me? There are loads of things in this life that are better to do than to think about. There are a whole lot of them that come to mind!

There's a difference between making thinking a vicarious replacement for action. You can see yourself being 40lbs thinner and healthier and exercising and having written a book and having married a beautiful woman and all of these things... but it's actually the process of getting there.

I meet people who say they want to have a good relationship and I tell them, *"Well, you need to meet 1,000 people so your odds of finding a really good one are increased. You need to have conversation of more than a minute. That doesn't mean you have to date them, but you really need to meet a lot of people. You got to kiss a lot of frogs to find a prince."*

Most people don't. Instead, they try to change somebody into somebody that matches a picture in their head. That doesn't work very well. Real motivation comes from having a really good plan and the plan has to include how to make yourself feel better as you do things. When you have food on your plate, if you have too much food, push part of it aside. Decide what you are going to eat and every bite you do, remember what it's like to be full so you can feel satisfied.

Most people don't realize we have built-in signals in the body. For example, sighing. I notice all the time when I'm eating with people. They'll sit back, sigh, and start to eat again even though the sigh was their body's way of saying, *"You're done."* If they paid attention to the signal and just pushed their food away rather than going back and picking at it and picking at it, then complaining they feel too full, they'd do better.

You can train yourself. I've hypnotized people and literally told them that if they eat more than a certain amount, they'll feel unpleasantly full. Oddly enough, they still do it. It feels worse than it did before. I thought at first that would be enough. But then I realized they needed to be able to chop off what they were going to eat in their mind and the closer they got to just eating that, the better they felt.

It wasn't the first bite. It was, *"I have three bites left, two bites, one..."* and then going, *"Wow! That's it. I'm done. No more. I'm feeling great!"* If you're moving towards feeling good rather than avoiding feeling bad, you set up a system in your mind where your passion builds as you do things. Relationships shouldn't start out great and get worse. They should be just the opposite.

The first time I got married, people said, *"Enjoy it now, because in a couple of years, it's going to be nothing but a ball and chain."* And I didn't even understand what they were talking about. I'd go, *"What do you mean?"* And they'd go, *"Well, at first, every-thing's great, but that wears off."* Excuse me? Painkillers wear off, but relationships shouldn't - they should get better as time goes along. If you're not planning that, it never happens.

Real motivation is a great plan. There's no excuse to not have one.

MOTIVATING YOURSELF

There are ways of thinking about things that work, just as there are things you say to yourself that work and things that don't. It's funny that somebody who can't clean the garage gets pumped up and goes out and bowls every Saturday night. They do this for a couple of hours, and they don't leave because they're tired of bowling. The closer they get to the end of the game, the more excited they get, the more they try to perfect their bowl. Golfers, the same. Yet they look at their garage and they go, *"I need to clean it someday."* One is achieving perfection, which builds passion, and the other isn't.

It's the same neurology. Your neurology doesn't care whether or not you set out a plan to clean out your garage and make everything look perfect, or to read a book from one end to the other. People go, *"Oh, I've half-read the book."* They start reading and it's laborious. What's the tone of the voice in their head like? Is it excited or does it sound like a five year old struggling through something? The nuance of detail is what makes something exciting versus not exciting. If your plan is to make an activity exciting and to feel better with everything you do that completes it, you'll be a person who manifests and finishes things in this life.

Otherwise, you simply won't. Oddly enough, the people who do well at one thing, do very badly at another. They don't realize the style of thinking is what counts, not the activity. It's not whether you're mowing your lawn or cutting your flowers or bowling or playing tennis or polishing your floors. It's not profoundly different.

If you look at your sink full of dishes and you go, *"Ugh! I don't want to do this,"* of course you're not going to. However, if with each dish you take out, wash, and put on the counter makes you feel better, then you'll strive to do it towards the end.

The whole notion of taking a feeling and spinning it is about increasing such feelings. When you think about things when you're excited and motivated, it starts in a place in your body, and it moves in a circular motion. It either rotates forward or it tumbles back, it goes clockwise or counter-clockwise.

I've been through this thousands of times with people and every time you ask them about things they're having trouble doing, it's going one way, and every time you ask them about the things that are easy, it's going another way. Even when people first get excited, they'll make a hand gesture and as time goes along, it slows down.

Learning to control the meter of your own passion and your own feelings so that they get stronger over time, even if they start to lull and knowing how to pump them back up, is discipline. That's the definition of discipline. Discipline is not something that's genetic, it's not like having red hair; it's a mental activity. You discipline your mind, focus your attention, and build up your feelings so you have the strength, the focus, and the attention so your neurology is singing in the right direction rather than dragging its feet backwards.

MOTIVATING PEOPLE AT WORK

In business, when you're a leader, you need to realize not everybody is motivated the same way. You can't do the same thing with everybody and have it work. People are different. Unless you get them all to think the same way or unless you only select people who think a certain way, you're going to have varieties of behavior. What you do with one person will be different to another.

One of the big mistakes leaders make is they don't have a loop where they're constantly checking to make sure things don't get too far behind. When you say, *"Have the proposal done in a week,"* you need to go in three days later and make sure they're halfway done. That's what a leader does.

A leader constantly provides the feedback for people to know where they are in the process, so they either extend the deadline because it's more work than anticipated or they get the person working harder or faster, or get them help. They may not know how to do it. A lot of people say, *"Yeah, yeah, yeah..."* but they don't actually know. When you're a middle management person or you're the CEO of a company, your job is to teach people how to do their job.

That's why it's so hard to replace a CEO, because when you grow up with a company, you know all the tasks that need to be done, whereas if you come in from the outside, you have no idea how things are put together. Therefore, to be able to work your way through a procedure so you make sure everybody is doing their job, whether it's a big corporation or a small business, you have to be able to have feedback loops about what's getting done. These loops might not always be directly with the employees, but are at least with the management or upper management people and make sure everything is getting done in the right way.

I remember the great hotelier Conrad Hilton was the first one to have people fill out those little questionnaires in hotels - *"How was your stay?"* He had them all sent to him and he would read through them to see how guests were feeling about his hotels. He wanted to have extra information. He didn't want to call the person running the franchise and go, *"How's everything going?"* and always get, *"Everything's great! Everybody loves the hotel."* Well, maybe they do, maybe they don't. The franchise owner is not going to tell you.

Hilton thought that although most people mightn't fill the form out, certainly the disgruntled ones would. He wanted to be able to adjust his hotels so he got fewer and fewer disgruntled people. That's smart. Smart is instead of trying to get everybody to approve of what you do, find out what you're doing that isn't working well enough and adjust it so it works better.

MOTIVATING CHILDREN

Motivating children is another question we've been asked many times. How do you best get them to go to bed, brush their teeth, clean up after themselves? Well, the key here lies in the strategy where you turn it into a game and when they're really young, you teach them to play it.

I used to train dogs, and what was really obvious was you didn't train a German Shepherd to go and beat somebody up, you taught them it was a game. You had agitators and if they went and knocked the guy off the fence, you threw the ball for them. So, it was reward-based. First, you got them real excited about chasing the ball. Then, pretty much, you could get them to go sniff out where the drugs where – sniff out this and sniff out that – and you rewarded them.

If you want your kid to want to brush their teeth, then you should put your toothbrush in their bathroom and sing a song or play a game they like. If you can get babies to play patty-cake with you, you can sing a little song and get your kid to brush their teeth with you. Pretty soon, you won't have to go in, they'll go in by themselves and start doing it.

Sometimes it's as simple as buying them a fancy electric toothbrush and telling them they're not old enough to use it yet, to the point where they really want to sneak in there and brush their teeth without you. It just requires you keep the goal in mind instead of thinking you can always threaten people into doing things, and making it worse by attaching bad feelings to the activity.

When I went to school, they made almost everybody hate math because teachers weren't really mathematicians. I can remember my teacher saying, *"Okay, put your art project down. It's time to do mathematics."* Their tone of voice was like, *"Uh, this is going to be drudgery."* This applied to them -they hated math, and they conveyed that to pretty much everybody. If you want kids to be excited about something, you need to be excited.

Think about when you went to school. You had a few teachers that were excited about stuff and they got you excited. When I was in the 6th grade, they had us all build jet airplanes out of Plasticine and put steel tools in the end of it. They had us doing all kinds of math to design wing size and speed resistance. They didn't call it algebra, they called it airplane design.

I remember kids asking me how you did the equations because I was a little better at math than most of them. Other kids who normally wouldn't have given a shit would go, *"This equation we got, what size should the wings be on my plane?"* Sitting down and doing the equation with them, they'd go, *"Wow! You put this in for the size and the surface area, and you do it by this and this, and it tells you how much drag is going to be on the plane."* Suddenly, math had meaning and purpose, and if there's a purpose to it, people will be much more likely to want to do it.

A three-year-old kid isn't going to think about losing his teeth when he's 40. That really isn't going to motivate him. If you keep telling him, *"If you don't brush your teeth, your teeth will fall out,"* it's not going to make much of a difference. A kid that age, his teeth are going to fall out anyway. Then, when their teeth fall out, they'll say, *"Oh, that wasn't that bad. I grew another one."*

The whole thing is to make it fun and the more you do it, the better you feel. Those are the things that we do more often. It's how our neurology is designed. When we reach out to pick up a glass, the closer we get to the glass, the faster our hand moves, the closer we are to achieving success. Once we make contact on the palm of our hand, we have to switch muscles and pull it back. Lifting the glass is always going to be slower than the moment before your lips because we accelerate mathematically towards success. It's what out neurology is designed to do. Neurology is designed so the more you know where the target is, the faster you go towards it.

DAY 11
TASKS

SPINNING MOTIVATION

- Think of something that makes you feel incredibly motivated, like doing your favorite hobby or eating your favorite food.
- Notice the feeling moving through your body.
- Spin this feeling stronger.
- Create an image of something you want to feel more motivated to do as you continue to spin the feeling of motivation.
- Keep doing this as you start to feel more compelled to engage in this behavior. So, for example, if you're very motivated to exercise, imagine how good you feel when you exercise and spin that feeling throughout your body.
- If you want to be more motivated to eat healthy then imagine yourself eating healthy while spinning the feelings of motivation you feel when exercising.

MAKING PROGRESS

Sometimes, it's easy to start something, but the challenge comes when trying to continue it. To handle this:

- Think of something that makes you feel incredibly motivated. Spin this feeling stronger throughout your body.
- Imagine a task that you are in the middle of doing.

Spin the feeling of motivation as you imagine yourself completing different parts of the task and build the motivation you feel along the way so the more progress you make, the more motivated you feel.

For example, let's say you're in the middle of writing a book. Find something that motivates you and build the feeling of motivation.

Then think about the different points along the way of writing a book like finishing each chapter and imagine feeling this feeling as you finish one chapter and start the next. By planning to feel motivated between chapters you ensure that you will continue writing until the process is complete.

ADAPTING TO DIFFERENT PEOPLE

When motivating other people, ask yourself what are the specific things that might motivate that particular person. For example, if someone works for you and you want to motivate them to work hard on a new project, what can you use or say to make them more motivated? Are they motivated by praise or autonomy or power or money? What works the best to get them to do their best work? How can you use it to get them to do so?

MAKE IT FUN

Children tend to be much more motivated by games than by normal hard work. By getting them to see it as a game, you are more likely to get them to do what they need to do. So, when motivating children, ask yourself how you can make the activity fun and how you can make it into a game.

For example, if you want your children to get their homework done, how can you make them see it as fun? What could you say or do that will make them think about completing homework as a game? This can work for you too! Once again, you get from the exercises what you put in.

The more you apply yourself to these exercises the more you will increase how motivated you feel day-by-day. It is also crucial that you learn to handle when things don't go according to plan. That's why next we will talk about resilience next.

DAY 12:

Building resilience

SCAN FOR VIDEO RESOURCES

R esilience is the quality of becoming more determined if things get more difficult or if things don't turn out to be the way you wanted them to be. Disappointment requires adequate planning. You have to know when to do it. A lot of people have quoted me on that, but I don't think they understand it's all about motivation. When something doesn't turn out the way you want it to, that's when you go back and make another plan and forge ahead.

There are two theories of how the universe came into being which leading physicists are arguing about now. I don't know that they're really profoundly different. One is the Big Bang - suddenly, there's nothing and BOOM! there's a lot of stuff! The other one is the Big Bounce - a universe collapsed on itself and re-emerged as what we call the Big Bang. The physicists have scientific reasons why they think one way or the other way.

To me, what we need in our life when things are not working is that Big Bounce. It should all collapse and come out with a new plan with greater determination. If something doesn't work out, it's because you're headed in the wrong direction with the wrong plan, so you need to pull your resources back to become even more determined to get where you want to go.

During the last recession in the US, lots of people who worked at companies for years were laid off as businesses downsized. They were lost; they had no backup plan. Simultaneously, their pension plan shrank in a crazy way because of the stock market. These are your choices: You either become depressed, apathetic, and you can give up, or you give it the Big Bounce: *"This is my chance to have an even better job, to start my own company, to do this, to make better use of my time so that nothing like this ever happens to me again."*

For some people, it was a dark hole in space and they fell down it like Alice through the rabbit hole, where they were at the mercy of everything that happened. Some people took it as the time to – BANG! – make a Big Bounce and make a new plan.

To me, this is the important thing: the greatest thing I've ever seen in human beings - in successful human beings that is - is determination. Not that bad stuff didn't happen to these people. The Apple co-founder Steve Jobs had a lot of bad stuff happen to him and came back from it; the great 20th Century entrepreneur John D Rockefeller had the same. It's like this with all of these successful people. Every time you read about their lives, something happened which took them down to the edge of nothing and they powered on back and became really rich. Whether you're talking about being a multi-billionaire or whether it's being a great musician who hurts his hand and can't play, that doesn't mean you can't write music, it doesn't mean you can't *play differently.*

I know a musician who lost one of his fingers, so he couldn't play the way he used to play. So, he started playing differently, he started leaving those notes out and it became a style of music. You either take difficulty and turn it to your advantage, or you take difficulty and you clobber yourself over the head with it over and over again. It's a simple choice. It's not as difficult as people think, but it's a question of how you mentally direct your energy. You're either making excuses or making pathways; things are either getting better or they're getting worse. There's not staying the same. People are either getting smarter or they're getting dumber. I've seen it for years that people who are getting smarter for a long time suddenly start getting really stupid.

This is going to happen to all of us. I'm not exempt from it. The question is: How short do you make the downhill climb? How long are you going to roll down the hill before you grab onto something and climb up again? You have to get to the point where you're fed up faster and you're more excited easier. Some people call this willpower, but I prefer determination. An act of will is really an act of determination. To me, it's just the ability to turn on the switch that makes you determined.

BECOMING MORE TOLERANT

It's also really important to be tolerant. Every time you're with somebody you could potentially argue with, who would poten- tially hire you or who would potentially buy from you, you need to be relaxed enough to stay calm. Every salesperson has to know how to have somebody come to them whose beliefs are diametrically opposed to theirs, who will say things that could even be offensive, and be able to stay relaxed and realize they can handle it.

The whole thing is, if somebody disagrees with you and you think it's really terrible, I always say inside my mind one sentence. I think to myself, *"Holy shit, I'm so glad I'm not this person. It must be really horrible to have such rigid beliefs."* I had somebody come to the door the other day, trying to talk me into a religion of some kind. If I had to worry about proving to everyone I was a Christian at every moment of the day, that would be a lot of work.

I hear people's coins drop on the ground. The art to having a calm confidence is being willing to listen to other people's coins drop on the ground, because when you're being interviewed by somebody and they make a snide remark, they just dropped their coins. Those are the moments of their life. Not only are they going to do it with you, they're going to do it to the next person, the next person, the next person. All of these wonderful moments that could have been special are splattering on the floor.

Every time you get unnecessarily angry you are dropping your coins. There are times to get angry, but most people get angry when it's just not useful, they yell at their kids about washing dishes and all kinds of dumbass shit. When your anger isn't directed at anything useful, you're just throwing your coins on the floor.

When you're wishing something would happen rather than making it happen, you're throwing your coins on the floor. When people are showing off or when somebody is interviewing you and they're dropping names and being a big shot, they're throwing the coins on the floor. With the amount of time it takes to interview somebody, you should *want* to know about them, get the information so you can pick the right person.

The United Stated has got 320 million people in it. If we'd picked the best person for every single federal job based on what the job really is, not based on whether they agreed with the person appointing them to the job, things would be hugely different. Instead, often people appoint those who agree with their point of view, not the most qualified person to do the job.

A CEO, somebody who's running anything, shouldn't pick people based on whether they know them because nepotism isn't the way to get good results. If you pick the absolute best person for a job, then things will change. This is what CEOs, presidents and people who run churches should do. You don't pick an accountant for a church because they're religious, you pick them because they're a good accountant; you don't pick a heart surgeon because he agrees with you on politics, you pick him because he will restore your heart.

If you pick a Supreme Court justice of the United States, they should be the person that knows the absolute most about the Constitution, it shouldn't be because they agree with your opinions. Their job is to interpret the Constitution of the United States, not interpret it your way. If you don't pick experts at things, you make things worse. It's like putting a politician in charge of an army – that's ridiculous! Armies have to have restraints and that's what politicians are for. A general should decide *how* a battle is fought, a politician should decide *whether* it's fought.

THE KEYS TO SUCCESS

Being successful is just like being healthy; you can't underestimate a good set of genes. Being in the right place at the right time helps. You just have to be the person who notices it. It's one of those things. Certainly, every one of us who has done something significant in the whole history and theory of knowledge and science has been in the right place at the right time.

If we weren't, nobody noticed. If it hadn't been for the work of the social scientist Gregory Bateson, I wouldn't have been able to do what I did; if it hadn't been for the linguist Noam Chomsky, it would've been a lot harder; if it hadn't been for certain socioeconomic events, there would have been challenges. All of us walk into these times and places. Gregory once said to me, *"We should have figured out what you figured 10 years earlier."* I said, *"You couldn't have. Chomsky hadn't written his books yet - it would've been impossible."*

Luck is being at the right place at the right time and noticing. You can pick 100,000 people and put them in the right place at the right time, and probably only one of them will notice. You have to make sure that you're the person that has the can-do spirit that says, *"Yes, we can!"* then do it.

If it's not working, you have to notice it and adjust it so it will. There are lots of people who have a bad plan and stick to it and it just gets worse. It has to be based on certain things. In business, it's got to be based on accounting; you've got to cut costs and increase profit. If you're spending more than you're making, you're not doing well. Our governments would notice that. You have to spend less than you take in to have a profitable business. Governments can print money, but then everybody's money is worth less. They make other people pay for their mistakes.

At the time of writing, it's amazing that in the United States we haven't had a proper budget for a while. You shouldn't run a household without a budget, let alone a country! To me, when you don't make good plans, bad things happen. Obviously, the deficit is bad and the national debt in most countries is utterly out of control. This is just bad planning. Whereas we may not be able to change what the government does about it other than voting for who we want in office, in our own lives we certainly can.

We need to have good budgets. We need to have good plans because you don't just budget money, you budget time, you budget energy, you budget focus on attention. People say, *"How do you know so much about so many things?"* Well, I read a lot. I read every magazine I can get my hands on, whether it's in my field or not, I read about all the different sciences and I study history. Part of the reason why I have a collection of postage stamps is because every one of those stamps marks an event in the history of a country. History can't really be altered as much as people think it can. You can describe it differently, but you can't alter what actually happened. Your opinion can be different, whether it was a good thing or a bad thing; what's treason at one moment is freedom fighting in another. To me, the key is to find that vehicle by which you get the most control of your life without having to control other people's.

HANDLING PERFECTION

Sometimes I hear people making excuses. *"It has to be perfect!"* or *"I'll do it, but I have to wait for X to happen first."* They will write the first line of their book and immediately delete it because it isn't the absolute best first line they can imagine.

These people fill the balloon and don't let out the energy. They think, *"if it doesn't match X, then I'm going to feel bad,"* instead of deciding it will make them more determined. If you go on a diet, start exercising and get to the end of the first week and haven't lost any weight, that's probably because you're losing fat and building muscle.

So, you should become even more determined to do it. There's a real difference between what's really happening and you setting a bar that goes, *"If it doesn't match this, I'm going to stop."* If you define what failure is (and all failure is a subjective definition), then you can get yourself to make excuses about anything.

Some people say, *"Oh, I'm a failure because I didn't lose 40lbs in a year."* Well, rather than saying you're going to lose 40lbs in a year, instead say, *"I'm going to lose 2lbs a week"* so that three weeks later, not losing anything makes you ferocious about it. You should exercise twice as much and eat a little bit less so you achieve your goal, because then, a week later, you can measure what's happening.

Instead of setting big goals and saying, *"If I can't achieve the whole thing, then why even bother?"* there's a smarter way. Your brain is just like a good car, if you buy a '57 Chevy and you want it to be cool, you paint it, you put big tires on it, you put chrome on the engine. Pretty soon, you'll have it better than it was when it came off the factory line – you pimp your car! And I'm trying to teach people to pimp their brains so the way they motivate themselves gets stronger in the face of adversity. Those are the people who really succeed.

If you read the history of successful entrepreneurs in the United States, it was never an easy ride. Things got the very worst when they became the most creative and when they stuck to their guns. If you don't keep a focus on where you're going to go and become a propulsion system that aims toward what you want, you won't get there.

It's not just that your passion is excitement, you have to be driven, you have to be freakin' determined. To me, determination is probably the most powerful human emotion because that's where you look at people achieving things. It's very satisfying. Somebody climbed Mount Everest for the first time, but it wasn't all fun. It was very difficult, but the more difficult it got, the more determined they got, and the more they fought for their goal because it feels good to be determined. It's not like party fun, but it is another good feeling.

When people are really determined and really set their minds to things, that particular kind of passion is just unrivaled. You see it in artists and musicians and all kinds of people who are driven to do something. No matter how many people tell them *"You can't,"* and no matter how many people say, *"You won't,"* or *"It's impossible,"* or *"Nobody will like it,"* or *"Nobody will understand it,"* they go do it anyway.

Believe me, I understand perfectly. Everybody told me I couldn't achieve what I set out to do, every time I set out to achieve something. *"Kid, you can't go and tell psychiatrists how to do things better."* No, actually you can. I did it over and over again because I was able to show them something they couldn't see because I figured out what it would take to convince them. Then, your age becomes irrelevant. When you say, *"I'm too young to do this; I'm too old to do this; I'm too fat do this"* you won't do it. People go, *"I'm too fat to do this exercise, it's too hard."* Excuse me - that's the very evidence to show you how much you need it.

When you look at TV shows with these people with enormous amounts of weight and they make them do nothing else but exercise for a year, you can see in all of them this sense of failure. However, there's a certain point at which the teacher just hammers them so much they finally become determined. You can just watch the scales turn. They start losing more weight, they start believing they can do it, and they start working harder. It becomes easier to work harder because the truth is, once you start to enjoy hard work, it's not work anymore.

DAY 12
TASKS

BOUNCING BACK

- Imagine in the future that you fail to achieve what you want to achieve.
- See yourself feeling the bad feeling and it instantly turning to determination.
- Imagine yourself bouncing back and immediately learning and moving on.

- Continue to imagine various scenarios where you aren't successful and, in each one, see yourself bouncing back and turning things around. For example, if you were learning to drive you could imagine failing the driving test and then straightaway going back to work on your driving until you pass it the next time. Whatever it is that you are attempting to do, the key is to train yourself to imagine taking failure on board as useful information that helps you to succeed.

FROM TOLERANT TO CURIOUS

When dealing with people with a vastly different perspective than you, begin to ask yourself questions about them and how they think. Become curious about how they think and why they think as they do. So often, we find ourselves trying to justify why we are correct instead of truly understanding others. Instead, search out people with different points of view than you and do your best to figure out how they reached the conclusions that they reached.

BEING READY FOR LUCK

Imagine yourself getting all the luck in the world with everything you do and immediately see yourself taking advantage of this luck. See yourself seeing everything that happens as an opportunity for success. Start looking for opportunities every time you leave the house. Imagine anything that happens serving you in some way and always ask yourself *"How could this be the luckiest thing to happen to me?"*

Building resilience is one of the single most important skills that you need to succeed in the modern world. It's essential that you do these exercises regularly so that you can train your mind to handle setbacks in the most effective way. It is now time for us to look at helping you to build the big plan for your life.

DAY 13:
The Big Plan

SCAN FOR VIDEO RESOURCES

It is because we know people will make mistakes along the way that we prepare for this. The big plan incorporates the possibility they might mess up and enables them to go back on the plan. The earliest thing I learned about working with people was to get them to imagine, in the future, the mistakes I knew they were going to make. Everybody would come back to me and say, *"Blah, blah, blah happened and so I stopped doing it. I started smoking again."* A couple would come in and they'd be fine for three weeks and they'd get in one fight and then just start fighting all the time. They all thought one mistake and the change was over. When they hit the mistake, they didn't see it coming, so it busted the generalization that said they'd changed.

Instead, build it in that you're going to diet for two weeks and then you're just not going to be able to stand it and you're going to eat a bag of potato chips. The question you'd be asking while you're eating the bag of potato chips is: *"Which potato chip am I going to stop and laugh and go, I'm slipping back into who I was, I better put them down and go back on the plan?"*

When you wake up in the morning, you have two choices: You either feel guilty, or you can think, *"Time to get back on the plan."* There's a board game called Monopoly, where each player tries to buy up property, and sometimes they can end up in jail. There's something called a *Get Out of Jail Free* card. When working with clients, I'd give them three cards and I'd say, *"Okay, you get one card a month"* (or two cards a month, whatever it was).

What was funny was when I gave them the cards, they were less likely to fuck up because they wanted to spend them wisely. That's why I think what we should do is give people *Fuck-up* cards, basically. Have them make *X* number of them so whatever their plan is, they get to use them. We tell them, *"You're going to get three of these in X amount of time,"* so if you get five a year or if you get two a month, you have a choice where to spend them. You can spend them on your diet; you can spend them on your exercise; you can spend them on this or spend them on that.

Suddenly, they have become a commodity; people start to think of time as a commodity: *"Oh, I've to spend that? It's just a bag of potato chips... I'd rather wait until I get to a restaurant and have a piece of cake and make it worth it."* I would say to them, *"You have to tear up the thing when you do it,"* and people would go to a restaurant and forget to bring it and they'd literally tell me, *"I was there, I was going to eat the cake, but I forgot my ticket. I thought, 'well, I'll do it next week'."*

> **In this chapter at the top right-hand corner of every second page, you'll see a card called Bad Picture. Inside the picture in the corner there is a 'Get out of Stupid Free' card. As you flick through the pages quickly, the Get out of Stupid Free' card will overtake the Bad Picture card. This is to remind you that you can start to change from the old pictures of you making mistakes and begin to think about getting a card that allows you to leave the mistake behind and continue with the change in behavior.**

BAD PICTURE

(when you notice you're
reverting back to bad
thoughts, feelings or actions)

**GET OUT OF
STUPID FREE
CARD**

If they're going to fuck up at something, I think fucking up at fucking up is the best one. It's funny how it's so difficult for people to think of time as a commodity when it's really the only commodity we get. I saw on the news the other night that a 16-year-old girl was run over on her bicycle. All everybody said was, *"She was so young. She was at the top of her class. Everybody loved her. She missed all of the good stuff in her life."* They all were going, *"I feel so bad for her."* I was looking and I was going, *"Well, she lived her whole life without hesitation. She was the best at everything she did; she was the valedictorian; she achieved one thing after another. Many people who were sitting around and talking about it didn't."* It's not until people are dead that they get it. You get a bag of time and you don't know big it is. So, how are you going to spend it? Drip, drip, drip...

You're either throwing coins on the floor or you're spending them wisely. You're even spending pennies on what you should spend silver dollars on. You go into an interview and you try half-assed - you're spending 50 cents on something you should spend $5 on. Your time is valuable; you need to decide when to do what you want to do. Sometimes flying on a plane economy mightn't matter to you, but other times you might need to get some sleep so you can work the following day. It's worth the extra money. You not only budget your money, you budget your time accordingly.

I had a client once who was changing a negative habit and I said to them, *"Now in the future, you may revert to this specific behavior once or twice and when you do, you'll immediately feel much more motivated to continue on with the new behavior."* What I loved about that was a lot of people think, *"I'm going to go off the cigarettes, or I'm going to stop. I'm going to go on a diet or go off a diet."* They think of it as on/off, so as soon as they make a mistake once, they're done.

As soon as they eat that first hamburger they go, *"I failed on the diet."* That's the way New Year's resolutions work: *"Oh, I'm back on the normal stuff."* So, they say, *"One cigarette and that's it, it's over!"* Whereas I get them to realize that when you project yourself in the future, you assume you're now living the new lifestyle - you've now become the new person. In order to revert to something, to revert to a specific behavior, it presupposes you're already living the new type of life.

Then you're preparing them that if they do revert, if they do get tempted with a cigarette, if they do eat the wrong kind of food, immediately that just serves to motivate them even more towards where they need to go. To me, that's one of the biggest things people don't get. When they try to overcome a problem, they see it as either on or off. Even things like panic attacks or things like fears are like, *"Oh, I feel scared again, therefore whatever I did didn't work."* It's the on/off dichotomy, whereas when you can get people to start thinking in terms of reverting and continuing where they left off, things change.

Disappointment requires adequate planning, but so does success. If you set up a thing where having one panic attack makes you decide what you tried didn't work (even though you just spent a week without an attack) rather than repeating what worked and having another week without an attack, that's just a bad plan.

BAD PICTURE

GET OUT OF STUPID FREE CARD

I'm sorry, but if you spent a lifetime engaging in stupid behaviors, especially when it comes to eating, having fears and things like that, you have to understand you may slip up, but that doesn't mean it's over, it just means you are getting there.

Feeling hungry when you are on a diet is a natural thing. If you can go five days and look at the cake, the fact that you feel you want it means you should diet; the same feeling is telling you to do a different behavior.

Your feelings don't force you to act. Knowing you crave something should be enough to tell you to not do it. See, craving can make you do it or it can make you not do it. The fact that you feel something is only the beginning and it has to do with the intensity of it. You learned on Day 2 how to turn feelings up and down.

People act like emotions are running wild. They talk about *controlling* emotions, not *using* them. You can make feelings stronger, you can make them weaker. It's really not very hard. The size of what you think affects the intensity of the feelings. Having 15 lessons tell you how to control feelings and how to ask good questions enables you to make long-term changes happen.

If you learn a little bit every day, then you can build in automatic habits. Over the years we've studied this stuff, it becomes a habit for us to ask other people the questions they don't ask themselves. And it's not like they're really that different. When people come in and say they feel bad about something over and over again, we ask them, *"How do you know when to do it?"* and they have to back up. They'll then tell us what they're thinking that produces a bad feeling, but that's not the important part of it. The important part is if you know *when*. You just need to get in front of it to know when to decide ahead of time. The big thing is, time is the currency of life and decisions about how you spend it are the important things. You're either going to spend it doing what you've always done, or you're going to make it where you learn to do something new. This requires practice.

When you practice stuff, even the world's best athletes don't perform perfectly every time. When they learn a new skill, it's as awkward as can be. They switch to a new bat, or a new tennis racquet, there's always going to be a learning curve. For you to learn to be happier every day, to be more motivated, to consistently go to the gym, to consistently be more polite to your wife, all those things people need to learn to do to be happier, only requires you start at the right time.

If you walk in the house and you're thinking about work, of course your wife feels unnoticed. It's just that simple. Walking through your door doesn't mean to you, *you're* home. This is a very easy thing to change in your mind, you just have to make a plan and you stick to your plan. If you screw up now and then, you remind yourself of what the plan is rather than go and blow the bad things out of proportion. The bigger the idea the more you remember it.

TIME MANAGEMENT

If people say they don't have enough time, the funny thing is they spend time worrying about it. If they spent the time they spend worrying about it actually doing it, it'd be done.

BAD PICTURE

GET OUT OF STUPID FREE CARD

It's because they didn't plan for it. They take a look at their time schedule and they go, *"It takes me all this time to do all these things, and I don't have time for this."* Well, how do you make time? By better time management. You cut out unnecessary things and you keep the things that are necessary.

I believe it was one of the Ivy League colleges which asked its alumni if they could have one thing to make them more successful, what would it be. The largest number of people answered an extra hour every day.

The truth is, you're probably wasting over an hour every day. You're probably wasting it by sleeping too much, by worrying too much. You waste it by thinking about what you could have done, and all of these spaces where you're not doing something are spaces where you could be.

Also, having a hierarchy of what's more important is crucial. Yes, of course you have to do certain things. You have to brush your teeth and take a shower, you have to commute to your job. There are certain things you need to do. However, there are a lot of things you don't need to do. If you really wanted to do something that takes a longer time, something that takes some discipline

- writing a book, painting a painting, learning to be a better artist – whatever it is, you have to slot it into your schedule.

It's like, there's somebody saying they haven't got time to go to the gym all the time. Then you ask them where the gym is and it's halfway across town. You've got to pick a gym close enough so you don't spend all the time you could spend exercising, commuting. Maybe pick one next to your job so you can stop on the way home or go at lunch?

If you're not looking for how to make things easy, but instead looking for why you shouldn't do them, you won't do them. You can ask *why?* about almost anything and people will give you an answer. You ask kids, *"Why didn't you clean your room?"* They come up with elaborate excuses, but the real answer is because they didn't want to.

You make it so they have a sense of pride over cleaning things. You don't do that by making it unpleasant by yelling and screaming at people; that's not how it's done. You've got to make it so that every task they complete, they get rewarded more than the task before it. When you do that, people build up positive sensations. You teach people to sing.

I worked once in a factory and they had an area in the assembly line that slowed down, so they hired more people. Even by adding or doubling the number of people, it still didn't move that much faster. When I walked up and down the assembly line, I realized it was the most boring part. Not that any of it was really that exciting, but it was literally sticking a pin in something. So, instead of scolding them and yelling at them and telling them to go faster, we tried something different.

The drudgery had literally been spreading from one person to another, so I made up a little song they could sing. I got them all to take a step forward and stick the pin in and sing this little song. I'd recorded it in my studio, and when I played it and I showed

```
BAD PICTURE

GET OUT OF
STUPID FREE
CARD
```

them how to do it, they all said it was ridiculous and stupid, but then they started doing it and laughing at each other.

You could watch the meter on the assembly line speeding up to the point where they got rid of six people and moved them to other things. The part that was singing started shifting to the other parts on the line. People started using the same rhythm to talk about their little part of the process. The whole assembly line started speeding up, and the only difference is that it became a pleasant activity rather than people going, *"Oh God, I've gotta do another one of these!"* They were anticipating it like it was a dance step.

The same people who claim they don't want to do something repetitive will go out and dance for hours in exactly the same way. Whenever I'm presented with a task, I ask, *"How can I enjoy doing this?"*

They had a lot of back injuries in a plant where people had to lift things, and they used to bring them in a room and scold them for lifting improperly. They would send people through and if they started to lift something improperly, they'd jump on them and scare the hell out of them. They'd criticize them. The more they did that, the higher the level of back injuries they got.

I was hired by the insurance company to come in to see if I could change it. In those days, we had 8mm film. All I did was put pictures of people lifting the same things they were lifting (with no sound) and projected it on the ceilings and on the walls, all over the place. I used some of the people from the factory doing it so whether or not they were looking at it consciously, it was in their minds.

Oddly enough, over a short period of time the number of injuries decreased because we put the right idea in people's minds at the right time. We didn't tell them and then send them back in. It was on the wall all the time, instead of a thing that goes, *"Don't make this mistake!"* it was a thing that said in the back of their minds – *"This is how it's done!"* They just saw it happening over and over again. At first, they looked at it and made jokes about it, but after a while, they stopped thinking about it and just started doing it. To me, motivation and getting people to behave in better ways has to get into their unconscious. And how do you teach people to unconsciously think more properly? Practice!

BREAKING THINGS DOWN

Every trip begins with a first step and that first step might be picking up the phone and booking an airline flight. You have to be able to set your goals and move backwards from that goal to where you are. If you say, *"I want to be able to do 30 chin-ups,"* and you weigh 400lbs, you won't even be able to make it to the first one and you'll say to yourself, *"I'll never get there."* However, if you ask the question, *"What do I have to do to be a person who can do this?"* then you're going to start to say, *"Well, I have to be stronger, I have to be lighter."*

You have to make it easier to pick up, so you go, *"What does it take to lose weight?"* Well, you have to burn more energy, you have to eat less and burn more calories. If all you did was deadlift you wouldn't lose weight, you'd build muscle mass. You'd lose fat, but you wouldn't lose any weight. If your goal is to do chin-ups, you want to be lighter, so you need to do cardio.

BAD PICTURE

GET OUT OF STUPID FREE CARD

You need to do things that burn off pounds without building tremendous amounts of muscle.

If you want to just be stronger, there are a lot of workouts athletes do that are designed to make them stronger. Consider a strongman contest. Imagine the determination it would take even for a strong person to lift the things these people lift. I have to tell you, there is no reason for you to pull a truck yourself, but these people become determined to do these things, they set their mind to it and they work all day, every day on it. They spend lots of hours. Even though it's hard work, they enjoy the hard work.

What's missing in most people's plans is to enjoy the difficulty of the task. The truth is, if it was really easy as *press a button* and succeed, then it wouldn't be as much fun to do it. The fact it takes a long time gives you a greater sense of satisfaction and a greater sense of self-control. When you start running your own mind and your own body and your own life, you will feel better about yourself and you'll feel better about everything in your life.

LEARNING TO PRIORITIZE

If you're going to prioritize, you have to prioritize based on your own life and where you want to go. You have to be able to go into the future. I know people who go into the future and see themselves having a big house. Actually, they don't see themselves - they see a big house, a beautiful wife and five kids. When you ask them, *"Are you in the picture?"* most of the time they go, *"Well, no, I'm looking at my life."* I go, *"But you're not in it,"* and they go, *"Well, I could see myself standing there."* I say, *"Really? I see you in a wheelchair, having had a stroke and the rest of them are living off the insurance money!"* You see, that is one way to get there; so you may as well see them standing around your graveside because you died and left them your life insurance.

It's the process of how you get there. If you pick a wife by how she looks, then you really need to get one that won't move or talk, because if you want to have interactions with a person, you don't know what it's going to be like until you're doing it. You have to learn how to enjoy that person's behavior for what it is. When you prioritize your life, you have to back up and say to yourself, *"This is where I'm going to start, this is where I'm going to attempt to go."* As you go along, you need to keep adjusting the goal so it fits what you really enjoy.

I know a lot of people who got into a business because that's what they thought their future was going to be, but they ended up studying for years. I know somebody who went all the way through college, all the way through law school, and got a job as an intern in a law firm. He came to me and he goes, *"I've discovered that I hate being a lawyer. All I do is read this stuff and write this stuff, and I don't like it. Someday, I'll be able to go to court, but I just don't like it. What should I do?"* I said, *"When you were going to law school, when you were doing this stuff, did you ever think about whether you liked it or not?"* And he goes, *"Well, I figured once I got out, it would be over."*

They actually train you to be a lawyer in law school, oddly enough. He went back and went to medical school because he figured out he would have rather been a doctor. To me, you shouldn't wait three years to prioritize. The fact his parents were wealthy enough to send him to both colleges, he was lucky. Most

```
BAD PICTURE

GET OUT OF
STUPID FREE
CARD
```

of us aren't that lucky. We need to go into the future and figure out if we want to live in this reality. We need to understand what the nuance of it is and start backing up and going, *"Where do I start?"* because you don't go to medical school until you've finished high school.

I meet a lot of young people going to college and you have to understand, young people face this dilemma. When you're five years old, a month lasts forever because it's such a large percentage of your whole life. When you're 60, not so much; a month goes by in the blink of an eye because it's less percentage of your life. When you're 18 years old, four years is just under a quarter of your life. It's almost a fifth of your life and so going to college for four years, it's very difficult to look in the future.

What people really need to do is go into college to find out what they want to be. They go in saying, *"I'm going to be a doctor like my dad."* Well, if they went to the office with him all the time and really knew what a doctor does, they might be right. However, they should also think about living the life itself. What's it going to be like in a hospital with sick people all day long? A good doctor explores to find answers; that's what diagnosis is, it's like a giant puzzle you have to solve. If you're not a person who enjoys puzzles, you either have to make yourself into one or you should pick something else.

The steps are to be able to take the big picture and be able to move back. As you're moving back, find out what activities you have to engage in, then make a decision about whether it's worth it. Now the trouble with that is when you're 20 years old, you don't have enough experience to make that judgement. Your calls can be wrong, but if they are you just adjust.

I know a successful business person in his 40s with a lot of money. One day, he walks in and says, *"I hate this!"* So, he went back to college, to medical school, and became a doctor. Oddly enough, eight years later he's one of the best doctors, whereas most people become a doctor when they're a lot younger.

Becoming a doctor when you're 50 isn't going to give you a long career unless you practice way into your 80s. However, he did one thing, and the one thing in his mind was, *"If I can do that well, I can do this well. This, I'll enjoy; that I didn't enjoy so much."*

Everything you do should be something you do with passion. When you go to college and you take a class and it's not really what you're interested in, you should get yourself interested and do the best job in it. When I got a job working in a supermarket sticking groceries in a bag, I made sure every bag I put the stuff in was methodical. I'd look at all the stuff that was going to come across that aisle and figure out how to put it together, so every bag would be perfect and nothing would be crushed. If I'm to spend the time doing something, I want to do it really well. I don't go, *"This I'll do well and this I won't do well."*

The more people have passion and discipline about every little thing they do, the better off they'll be with the important things. I have good relationships that last a long time. That's because if they're not good relationships, I stop them. I've had people who were supposed to be my friends and they didn't act like it, so

BAD PICTURE

GET OUT OF STUPID FREE CARD

I just stopped being friends with them. They would come back and go, *"Why did you cut me off?"* I don't even try to explain it to them. If they treated me unfairly, why would I expose myself to it again? That's just silly. So, I may not have a lot of friends, but I have good friends. I enjoy their company. That's how it should be: a sense of discipline about the quality of your own experience, no matter what you're doing.

If you can't afford to do something you really enjoy, maybe you won't do it often. Wait until you can do the thing you want rather than do five other things you don't enjoy. If you take vacations to places you don't want to go to, they're not really vacations. I'd rather wait two years and work a little bit harder and actually go someplace I want to go.

DAY 13
TASKS

BREAKING THINGS DOWN

Focus on the goals you have set for yourself in your future. Start to break things down and decide specifically what you need to do and when in order to achieve these goals. Be clear of precise timelines and deadlines so you can see yourself achieving them step by step.

You can do this by going to the end, having successfully achieved your goals, and working backwards. Ask yourself, in order for this to have happened, what needs to have happened? What's the last step you'd need to take? The second last step? Keep moving backwards and create a series of short movies that go back from the goal to the present. This will highlight what needs to be acquired along the way.

Often, when we try to plan forwards we get lost along the way or find ourselves believing it mightn't be possible. By reverse engineering it, we can avoid this trap. For example, if your goal is to stop smoking, ask yourself what would need to be true in order for you to be a non-smoker. Imagine yourself being offered

BAD PICTURE

GET OUT OF STUPID FREE CARD

a cigarette and saying no. Imagine experiencing withdrawal and realizing it only took a couple of weeks. Imagine handling the withdrawal by changing your feelings. Imagine telling yourself with certainty that you're doing the right thing. Imagine building the belief that you can do it. Imagine before that making the decision to stop smoking.

Another example might be if you plan to learn a new language, like Italian. Imagine yourself in Italy speaking with the locals. Next, imagine yourself finishing the course you took and doing the exam. Imagine struggling with some of the vocabulary or grammar along the way but persisting and disciplining yourself to practice regularly. Imagine yourself beginning to take classes in Italian. Then imagine yourself building the belief that you could speak fluent Italian. Finally, imagine yourself making the decision to learn Italian.

ENJOYING PROGRESS

Imagine yourself achieving your goals and really enjoying the entire process. Vividly see yourself going through each step of your plan and smiling happily as you do. See what you'd see. Hear what you'd hear. Feel how you'd feel. Make it more colorful. Make the sounds louder. Feel the feelings more intensely.

GET OUT OF STUPID CARDS

Buy a few sheets of card paper. Print a selection of tickets or cards on these pages. Each ticket should be called a 'Get out of Stupid Free' card and look like this:

GET OUT OF STUPID FREE CARD

Consider the specific changes that you want to make in terms of your behavior and thinking. Give yourself three cards for each change. This means, if you revert to the old behavior, you will spend one of the cards. You give yourself a couple of chances to mess up along the way, but you only have three cards, so you must use them sparingly. On the back of each card, write *"You deserve another chance."*

For example, if you're changing your diet and cutting out candy, the temptation to eat it may occasionally arise. If it does and you falter, you spend a card. This means that instead of beating yourself up, you can instantly go back to living your life free from candy as you've been given another chance.

HANDLING MISTAKES

- Imagine in your mind reverting to the old behavior and instantly becoming super-motivated to get straight back to the new way of doing things.

GET OUT OF STUPID FREE CARD

- See an image of yourself, time and time again, getting straight back to the new positive and empowering behavior. Vividly imagine it.
- Make it into a movie that plays over and over again. For example, if you want to stop smoking you could see yourself reverting to cigarettes and, instantly, throwing the cigarette away and becoming even more determined to be a non-smoker.

LIFESTYLE PLANNING

Consider who you want to be in the future and what kind of lifestyle you want to engage in then. Make sure that the decisions you make are taking you down a road that will make you happy. Consider yourself six months from now, a year from now, three years, five years, 10 years and 20 years and notice what kinds of decisions make you live the kind of life that you desire. Be as clear as you can about exactly what you want to have happen in your life over the various time periods. Ask yourself what decisions would need to be made in order to these things to happen:

THE HAPPINESS CHECK

Consider the things in your life that make you happy in the long-run. Consider those that don't. Resolve to keep those things that you enjoy in your life and get rid of those that don't. For example, there may be people or things (drugs/toxic behaviors) that make you feel good in the moment but bad for a while afterwards. Be aware of the difference between something that feels good temporarily and something that is good for you and makes you feel good long-term. Spend time on the things that work for you long-term.

SHORT-TERM GOOD FEELING

LONG-TERM GOOD FEELING

Making your big plan work, however, requires you to make sure you are thinking in the best way possible. Something that will certainly help you do this is for you to work on your nutrition, which is what we will tackle next.

Day 14 is about what we call fueling the machine. Your body is run by what you feed it. Your brain operates best when your body has adequate nutrients. Since we are not qualified to talk about nutrition, we decided to go to the best expert in nutrition we know – Dr. Glenda Bradstock, who writes this chapter for us.

SCAN FOR DAY THIRTEEN WORKSHEET

DAY 14:

Fueling the Machine

by Dr. Glenda Bradstock

SCAN FOR VIDEO RESOURCES

There is a huge amount of information out there on nutrition and the kind of foods you need to eat to make sure your brain is in peak condition. In this short chapter I'm going to give you some basics, so that you can make a plan and start carrying it out immediately.

NUTRIENTS FOR THE BRAIN

Fueling the machine means learning how to make sure that you put into your body what your brain needs to perform in the best possible way.

Your body is like a machine - like a car. The engine of a car needs gasoline and oxygen to run, oil to lubricate, and clean spark plugs that fire on time to function properly. Your body, to operate optimally, gets its fuel by consuming foods with protein, carbo-hydrates and fats which provide vitamins, minerals and enzymes. Your brain runs best when you feed your body well.

EAT OFTEN

It's really essential to have frequent meals. Most people think of three meals a day as a good plan. Some people skip breakfast and eat a huge dinner. However, it's better to eat throughout the day every few hours. Three moderate meals, a snack between each meal and another at bedtime allow you to maintain a good blood sugar level. Normal blood sugar means your brain has constant fuel to allow you to think properly.

PROTEIN

Your body needs high quality proteins found in fish, chicken and other kinds of meat to stay have a ready supply of amino acids. Vegetarians and Vegans can combine foods like grains, beans, corn, pulses and soy protein to provide amino acids which are the building blocks for tissues, organs, muscles, skin and hair. These amino acids are also important as they help to form neurotransmitters – the chemicals that help transmit the signals between the synapses and allow messages to travel throughout the brain.

CARBOHYDRATES

You also need carbohydrates, which range from low-carbs such as broccoli, spinach and squash to high-carbs like sweet potatoes, white potatoes, bananas and peaches and grains. Carbs give you quick energy.

FATS

A balanced diet also needs good fats such as olive oil for low heat cooking, coconut oil for high heat cooking and avocado oil. Avoid sunflower, safflower, canola and corn oil. Oils give you fuel for prolonged energy.

Omega-3 fatty acids are found in fatty fish like salmon, tuna and mackerel are great for boosting memory, focus and brain health.

Omega-3 helps to reduce inflammation. Since the "American Diet" delivers more Omega-6 than Omega-3, I recommend taking a quality fish or krill oil supplement to guarantee getting sufficient amounts of Omega-3.

WATCH YOUR BALANCE

Proteins, carbohydrates and fats break down at different speeds. Carbohydrates break down first starting in the mouth. Proteins break down more slowly and fats break down even slower over as much as four hours. The amount of protein in a good serving is about the size of the palm of your own hand. Each portion of raw vegetables should be a full cup, while a portion of cooked vegetables should measure a half a cup.

VARIETY

With fruits and vegetables, when you eat from every color of the rainbow, it assures that you get a wide range of all the vitamins and minerals the foods of those colors can provide. The colors of the fruits and vegetables come from flavonoids which offer antioxidant and anti-inflammatory benefits which promote brain health. Choosing different foods is important so that you get the full range of enzymes to digest all the different foods.

SUGARS

The brain uses about 80% of the available glucose in the bloodstream. The more intensely you use your brain, the more glucose your brain uses for fuel. Listening intensely to a lecture and taking notes will burn more glucose than relaxing on the beach. A natural source of sugar is fresh fruit as a great energy booster for the body and brain. For sustained energy and normal blood sugar, it is good to pick something from the suggested snacks below.

BASIC VITAMINS AND MINERALS

Vitamin A is excellent for the skin, eyes, hair and wound healing. It is fat-soluble, so it is good to take it with an oil like olive or coconut to help transport it into the body. Foods that are yellow or orange such as carrots and squash contain Vitamin A.

Vitamin B gives you energy and is linked to the flora in your intestines. B Vitamins are found in a variety of fruits, nuts, wholegrains and meats to name a few. Gut flora produce B Vitamins and help you get the most out of the food you eat. The brain-gut relationship is well recognized. Good flora should outnumber the bad flora. When we eat sugars and breads, we feed the bad flora and they begin to outnumber the good flora. Antibiotics kill off both bad and good flora. So, to protect your gut and your brain, take a supplement in capsule form with billions of flora or a liquid product like Yakult or Kefir.

Vitamin C is great for the immune system. It is beneficial in stressful situations as it helps the blood carry more oxygen which, in turn, feeds the brain. Vitamin C rich foods include broccoli, spinach, tomatoes and citrus fruits.

Vitamin D is coming to the forefront in research right now for its connection to depression prevention. In order to get enough Vitamin D you have to be out in the sun with 75% of your skin exposed for 20 minutes a day, year round, but that is impractical. So, I recommend you seek out foods like fish, cheese or eggs to name a few and take a Vitamin D supplement.

Vitamin E is important to the skin, wound healing, heart function and vessel wall strength. You can find Vitamin E in almonds, spinach and sweet potatoes.

Vitamin K can be found in green leafy vegetables, animal products and fermented foods. It is important for blood clotting and bone strength, heart health and it boosts brain function. It is also produced by the good gut flora.

MINERALS

Minerals are like the spark plugs in the car analogy; they are the catalysts that start the biochemical chain reactions to make the body function.

Calcium is found in milk, kale and broccoli. It is important for bone formation and plays a part in pain control. Bone stores calcium as a reserve to supply calcium to the blood when the calcium level gets too low.

Chromium and selenium both help to regulate blood sugar which is important for brain function. You can find chromium in whole grains, pears, shellfish and nuts. Brazil nuts, fish, ham, pork, baked beans, and spinach are good sources of selenium.

Iron is found in liver, pulses, beans, nuts and seeds. It is part of the haemoglobin molecule which transports the oxygen in the bloodstream. Your brain needs oxygen, so it is critical that you get enough iron.

Magnesium is important for the heart as well as for muscle relaxation. It affects blood pressure. Recent research has found that magnesium also promotes memory and learning functions of the brain. You can find it in almonds, avocado, cashews, bananas and pumpkin seeds.

Potassium, along with sodium, regulate water balance and the acid-alkaline balance in the blood and tissues. It is critical in keeping the heart pumping regularly and for a healthy nervous system with normal nerve impulses. Potassium functions in the synthesis of protein from amino acids and in carbohydrate metabolism. Heavy perspiration depletes the minerals and can causes dehydration which can lead to serious medical conditions. Salmon, avocado and apricots are good sources of potassium. Brazil nuts, cottage cheese, eggs and brown rice are good sources of selenium.

Manganese is important for the soft connective tissue, ligaments and joint surfaces promoting smooth movement. It is also involved in hormone production and improved cognitive function and memory. You can find manganese in green beans, mustard greens, berries, whole wheat, brown rice and almonds.

Phosphorous's main function is the formation of healthy bones and teeth, but it also has a role in fat and carbohydrate metabolism. It is needed to make proteins to build and maintain the body. Phosphorous is found in fish, pork, tofu, milk, chicken, lentils, beef and whole grains.

Zinc plays a role in digestion, the nervous, immune, reproductive and skeletal systems. You can find it in high protein foods like meats, seafood and dairy, as well as in grains and legumes.

APPROACHES TO A PERSONALIZED DIET PLAN

There are various systems for determining the diet that is right for you – one is based on your blood type and another is based on your genetics.

Eating right for your blood type looks at your blood type as an indicator of your ethnic background. Most blood types are related to different regions of the planet where your ancestors lived and fed off the foods available. Your ethnic background affects the shape of your teeth, the length of your digestive and intestinal tracts.

The idea is to structure your diet so that it is compatible with your blood type. In the book Eat Right 4 Your Type by Peter D'Adamo you will find charts of what foods to eat or avoid depending on your type.

For example a type A should consume mostly vegetables, fruit, tofu, seafood and whole grains, whereas a type O does well on high protein foods - meat, vegetables, fish and fruit. It's a nice starting point for planning what's best for you to eat.

Genetics is also worth considering as an approach to diet. Products like 23andMe and AncestryDNA.com offer testing by taking a cheek swab and sending it in for your unique DNA. When you get the results back, they are very informative, but in broad strokes.

I have discovered a company named Genomics and the associated Neurobiologix. Instead of the multitude of genes they could test, they look for certain groups of genes focusing on inflammation, myelination, detoxification, hormone production and more. They can make specific dietary recommendations based on your genetic results. Neurobiologix also has formulated supplements to help you improve each situation you may have. If your body is healthy, your brain is going to be healthy. If you are free of pain in your body, you can think more clearly.

Also worth noting, there are numerous studies that have shown the benefits of a Mediterranean style diet in improving cognitive performance and mental clarity. This diet puts emphasis on fresh fruits and vegetables, whole grains, beans and legumes, nuts and seeds, healthy fats, fresh herbs and spices. This diet is also rich in fish and seafood as well as poultry, eggs, cheese and yogurt.

Care of the brain is also important along with feeding it the proper foods. Caring for the brain involves proper hydration, maintaining a healthy pH level, relaxation, breathing, exercising the body, stimulating the brain, getting social interaction and sleep.

Hydration Drinking clean, filtered alkaline water is important to your health. Drinking a lot of water at one time is not helpful. Sipping on water throughout the day is the best. Consuming one ounce for each two pounds (one kilo) of body weight throughout the day is a good target to shoot for. Increase that amount to 4 extra ounces every 30 minutes at times of high temperature or intense exercise. Curtail water consumption just before, during and after meals to avoid diluting the acids and enzymes in the mouth and stomach that are necessary to properly digest your food. Dehydration can cause lack of concentration, confusion, irritability, dizziness and anxiety. Inadequate water can interfere with the elimination of toxins from the body.

pH If your system is too acidic, you can feel agitated and anxious. Coffee, medications, and proteins process leaving an acid ash in the body. When your pH is too acidic, the alkaline minerals get used up trying to neutralize the acid to a normal pH. This depletes the stores of minerals for healthy heart and brain function. Vegetables and fruits increase the alkalinity in the body and replenish the stores of minerals. Eating more alkaline foods is a better plan to help the nervous system remain consistently calm. Some foods are neutral such as brown rice.

OTHER FACTORS THAT PLAY A PART IN BRAIN HEALTH

Relaxation Try getting out of town or away from work and away from stressful situations when you can. If that is not possible, start a mindfulness practice – closing your eyes and breathing deeply for a few cycles. Inhale through the nose for 5 seconds, hold the breath for 6 seconds, then exhale slowly for 7 seconds through the mouth. This will shift you from a sympathetic fight or flight mode to a parasympathetic rest and relaxation mode.

Stretching by reaching to the ceiling, then bending to touch your toes will help to relax the muscles themselves and improve your circulation. When you stretch, hold each stretch for 10 or more seconds, stretching a little further with each breath. Never bounce during a stretch.

Breathing properly is essential for optimal brain function. Many people breathe in a shallow way only filling the upper third of the lungs. You can test this by lying down on your back and balancing something light like a box of Kleenex on your stomach. Retrain your awareness as you breath and make the box go up and down and become more conscious of how your diaphragm helps to fill your lungs completely. Effective breathing is essential for good circulation and detoxification, ensuring your brain is working in the best way possible.

Exercising the Body Research shows exercise makes our brains work better and improves our thinking, memory and learning. Intensive aerobic exercise for 30 minutes at 60% to 75% of your maximum heart rate two times a week will increase BDNF – brain derived neurotrophic factor – which prevents death of brain cells, induces growth of new neurons and synapses and supports cognitive function. Stress reduces BDNF. Power walking, taking a couple of flights of stairs or parking away from entrance to work give you opportunities to get in little bursts of exercise. Even 40 minute walks, three times per week, promote the enlargement of the the Hippocampus, the memory center of the brain.

Stimulating the brain Exercising the brain is as important as exercising the body. Whether doing crossword puzzles, learning new vocabulary, new technology, new dance steps or watching quiz shows on TV, you're helping your brains synapses fire faster and more efficiently which impacts healthy function. Check out BrianHQ.com for some brain exercises.

Social interaction We are social animals and interacting with a diverse social network of friends and loved ones improves the plasticity and cognitive functioning of the brain. Relaxing and laughing increase oxygen to the brain and lower cortisol levels. Try taking a leisurely walk with a friend or a trip to an art show or museum.

Sleep The importance of sleep for good brain health cannot be overstated. It's not just the quantity of sleep that matters, but also the quality. While you're asleep, your body is busy rejuvenating itself. Numerous studies have shown that poor sleep leads to poor mental performance. Getting adequate hours of sleep is critical also because the brain detoxifies during sleep. During sleep a magical neuro-architectural event occurs, where the new learnings of the day are stored in your memory.

For a better night sleep try an ole wives remedy of drinking warm milk at bedtime for a dose of magnesium to relax the muscles. Epsom Salts dissolved in a warm bath before bedtime allow magnesium to be absorbed through the pores. Stretching helps to relax the muscles as well.

Get into the right frame of mind before bed by eliminating telephone calls, computer use and stimulation from TV. Reduce the exposure to blue light which activates the brain. The key is to train your body to get into a routine by going to bed and waking up at set times seven days a week.

MEAL PLANNING

Go to the grocery store and walk through the vegetable section and just notice the different colors of vegetables. Pick out about 7 of a variety of colors. Be adventuresome – add a new vegetable you've never tried.

Go into the fruit section and pick out 5 of your favorite fruits of different colors and add a new fruit to try.

In the meat/fish area pick out 4 different types of proteins, e.g., beef, chicken, pork chop, and salmon...

In the dairy section, pick out a large container of plain greek yogurt, some cream cheese, a dozen eggs, full fat cottage cheese and find a liquid probiotic, e.g., Yakult or Kefir.

Next are some suggestions for meals and snacks to help you get started on this new Adventure.

BREAKFAST IDEAS

Smoothie of almond milk, a scoop of pea protein or whey protein, a handful of cut up fruits or berries, a scoop of yogurt and some stevia or ½ a banana to sweeten if you need it. You can always throw in a pinch of cinnamon, some vanilla extract or turmeric just for some different flavors.

Sometimes, adding ¼ to ½ an avocado, some thick coconut cream or a 10-15 nuts, adds smoothness and richness to the smoothie.

The American standard breakfast: 2 eggs, some quality whole grain toasted bread, and even 2 slices of bacon.

Egg and zucchini frittata topped with parmesan cheese.

Cooked Grains like steel cut oatmeal, Wheat

Berries, buckwheat, quinoa, Couscous along with some coconut oil, cinnamon, chia seed powder or Flaxseed topped with some fruit and nuts.

LUNCH IDEAS

Tuna fish salad with romaine lettuce, cherry tomatoes and other raw vegetables and a ½ piece of fruit.

Piece of baked chicken with green beans sautéed in olive oil with pine nuts; shredded carrot salad with raisons and pineapple held together by a dab of yogurt.

Grilled or baked Pork Chop with baked sweet potato and raw spinach salad with olive oil and lemon juice for dressing; 1/2 of a green apple.

2 cups of soup made with some of all the vegetables on hand and some of chicken cut up in bite sizes. Try a chicken bone broth as the base; one clementine.

DINNER IDEAS

4-8 oz baked, broiled or grilled Salmon seasoned with lemon juice and salt; ½ Brussel sprouts tossed in olive oil, salt and pepper and baked;

½ cup of brown rice.

1 ½ cup of stir fried tofu and your choice of vegetables seasoned with a little curry powder; a ½ cup of Couscous.

4-6 oz filet Mignon grilled or broiled, mixed green salad with carrot, cucumber, celery, cherry tomatoes, chopped walnuts with a 1 ½ teaspoon each of olive oil and balsamic vinegar; a cooked vegetable of your choice.

In taco shells or pita bread create a great

Combination of some of the vegetables and some of the cooked protein or tofu topped off with salsa or yogurt.

SNACK IDEAS
(for between Breakfast and Lunch and Lunch and Dinner)

3 tablespoons of hummus with raw cut up celery, carrots, zucchini, yellow squash, red or yellow bell peppers, broccoli, cucumber or even red cabbage.

1-2 tablespoons of almond butter spread on celery stalks.

2 tablespoons of cottage cheese with a ½ piece of fruit.

10-12 nuts of your choice.

1/3 of a cup of blueberries with ¼ plain Greek Yogurt.

5 dried apricots with 8 walnuts.

¼ avocado mixed with vinaigrette dressing.

4 oz of a protein shake with blueberries, raspberries or strawberries.

All of these various food types and this kind of diet will play a big part in how well your body and brain function. It's essential to practice the art of eating on purpose so that you put yourself in the best possible position.

DAY 14
TASK

The task I am going to suggest in this chapter is a little different than the others. Making a change to how you fuel your brain is largely dependant on how well you adjust your lifestyle. So, instead of just doing one or two things, try incorporating each of the following into your daily plan. When you start to put them all together, you will notice a measurable improvement of not just your health but how effectively you can think on purpose.

EATING DISCIPLINE

Create different food plans for yourself based upon what you've learned in this chapter. Make sure the food plans incorporate the variety of different nutrients that you need for your brain. Have a look at the suggestions I have outlined above to give you some ideas.

MY FOOD PLAN:

DAY 1

BREAKFAST

SNACK

LUNCH

SNACK

DINNER

DAY 2

BREAKFAST

SNACK

LUNCH

SNACK

DINNER

DAY 3

BREAKFAST

SNACK

LUNCH

SNACK

DINNER

DAY 4

BREAKFAST

SNACK

LUNCH

SNACK

DINNER

DAY 5

BREAKFAST

SNACK

LUNCH

SNACK

DINNER

DAY 6

BREAKFAST

SNACK

LUNCH

SNACK

DINNER

DAY 7

BREAKFAST	
SNACK	
LUNCH	
SNACK	
DINNER	

DAY 8

BREAKFAST	
SNACK	
LUNCH	
SNACK	
DINNER	

DAY 9

BREAKFAST	
SNACK	
LUNCH	
SNACK	
DINNER	

DAY 10

BREAKFAST

SNACK

LUNCH

SNACK

DINNER

DAY 11

BREAKFAST

SNACK

LUNCH

SNACK

DINNER

DAY 12

BREAKFAST

SNACK

LUNCH

SNACK

DINNER

DAY 13

BREAKFAST

SNACK

LUNCH

SNACK

DINNER

DAY 14

BREAKFAST

SNACK

LUNCH

SNACK

DINNER

DAY 15

BREAKFAST

SNACK

LUNCH

SNACK

DINNER

STRETCHING

Schedule in a five to ten-minute stretch every morning, every evening and whenever you can during the day, ensuring you stretch your body and loosen up every muscle.

SLEEP

Create a sleep routine every night where you gradually wind down and cut out electronics. Teach your body when it's getting near sleep time. Identify some of the things that you are going to do every night to get better quality sleep based upon what you've learned above:

_____

_____

_____

_____

_____

BREATHING PRACTICE

Take ten minutes out of each day where you can practice your breathing using your diaphragm in the way explained above. Every once in a while during the day, notice how you are breathing and adjust it on purpose.

EXERCISE OPPORTUNITIES

Look for opportunities to exercise in your everyday life. Try parking further away from work, for example so your walk is longer. Identify five ways that you can regularly incorporate more exercise into your everyday tasks:

_____

_____

_____

_____

_____

EXERCISE

Schedule in three or four times each week that you are going to exercise. Make sure you allocate a specific time and location and type of exercise for each session and put it into your timetable for the week:

MONDAY (_____)

TUESDAY (_____)

WEDNESDAY (_____)

THURSDAY (_____)

FRIDAY (_____)

SATURDAY (_____)

SUNDAY (_____)

SCAN FOR CHAPTER FOURTEEN WORKSHEET

DAY 15:

Becoming smarter

SCAN FOR VIDEO RESOURCES

On our final day, we want to talk about becoming smarter. In psychology, we have something called the confirmation bias. The writer and futurist Robert Anton Wilson talked about it as "whatever the Thinker thinks, the Prover proves." We look for evidence that proves what we already believe, and we dismiss evidence that contradicts us. This is often something that causes a lot of people problems. The billionaire investor Warren Buffet says it's one of the reasons investors lose money. They're looking for what they think is a good idea, and they're looking for evidence to prove it rather than actually looking at the evidence. How can we actually use our brain to think more intelligently? How can we do this and not be stuck letting our own beliefs dictate how we feel to the world?

You have to have a device built-in. I try to build in a thing so every time people get back to where they feel uncomfortable, I get them to start laughing. This is better than just getting people to accept themselves. This whole notion from psychology I keep hearing about, especially that whole human potential movement, is you have to accept yourself the way you are. I've never bought into that because if you accept how you are, you're committing to your stupidity.

In fact, when you call stupidity a pathology and give it a name so you go, *"Okay, I'm having an anxiety attack,"* it becomes a thing rather than the process of anxiously thinking about stuff over and over again. Not only that, saying it out loud makes things different - *"I'm planning on doing it for the next 10 years!"* As soon as I say it like that to somebody, they go, *"Well, I'm not really planning."* I go, *"I know, because if you were planning, this wouldn't be what you planned."* They go, *"But I can't stop myself,"* and I go, *"Yes, I know. You have a plan and you're following it."* The fact that you can predict where you do these things and those things, where you will be afraid – *"Oh, it takes spiders! No, it's not spiders, it's elevators. No, it's not elevators..."* - this means you have an advantage.

When a guy says to me, *"I'm too nervous to go to talk to a woman,"* I know something about this. When one is there and they think thoughts that make them nervous, they're right. So, they keep going, *"Well, this is going to be like this forever."* They accept it instead of going, *"This is really stupid!"* The trouble is, people don't change until they go through thresholds. You have to look at what is, you have to see yourself doing the stupid thing and make that picture bigger and bigger until it just feels idiotic and you just laugh at it. As soon as you're laughing at it, it changes.

As soon as you laugh at being afraid of something and you're fed up with being afraid of going up in an escalator, then you're looking at an escalator and yourself and you're feeling something different. The trick is you can't stop where you think now - you must go further. If you stop at where you create the anxiety, you stop where the fear is instead of getting there and just running the memory backwards or shrinking it down.

I have people take bad memories they think of every day, shrink them down to the size of a quarter, and blink it black and white. Then, when they start to think about the memory, it happens by itself because they're going down the neuro-cortical pathway, they get to where it normally just gets stuck. If you just go anywhere else, it's better. It doesn't even have to be meaningful, just somewhere else. You can do this to the point where you don't stop on a bad thought.

When you stop on a bad thought and keep making it bigger and bigger, it keeps getting worse and worse, whereas if you just go anyplace... I mean, I could just go to point **A** and back, but instead of going to point **A**, I go to point **B** and back to point **A**. For example, think of going in the water and a shark chewing you up, and then suddenly you get un-chewed, spit out into a whole person, and swim back to the shore. This has a powerful effect! Neuro-synaptically, this is going to happen at the speed of light and if you do it over and over again, your brain will just keep doing it.

That's what the brain does, it repeats stuff, it makes it familiar and keeps going. So, if you think way beyond where you get stuck and you do it several times, your brain rewires itself.

I've had people who have terrible problems. A woman I worked with - when she was late, she had a psychotic episode. All I had her do was think of someone being late, and white it out like a brightness knob on a TV. I had her do it five times. Then when people were late, when she'd start to think about it, it would just white out in her mind.

I didn't look at it as a pathology, I just looked at it as stopping in the wrong place. If she just made it go white, she didn't go into the psychotic episode. The doctor said, *"Well you haven't treated the problem."* Actually, I have. The problem is now gone because neurologically she doesn't stop in a place where her neurology is defeating her ability to enjoy life and be functional. The purpose of an organism is to adapt to the environment. If the organism isn't adapting to the environment in a way that is productive, if it's just adapting in a way that's repetitious; that's not really thinking.

If you're going to remember, there's lot of good stuff to remember. So, if you're remembering bad stuff and it's immobilizing you, that's not smart. If you date a girl and she's always cheating on you and breaking your heart, and you keep going out with her over and over again, you're not remembering; you're not remembering this isn't working out. Whether it's a guy or a girl, if they keep repeating that behavior, there's got to be a point where you go, *"This is not productive."*

You need to find someone who is good for you. There are people who break up with someone after 30 years. Or their husband walks out on them and they keep thinking about the life that was good when it's not there anymore – they spend time wishing it was. This happens with people when their loved ones die. People go, *"I can't be happy, my husband died!"* I say, *"How long were you married?"* "Five years. He had a heart attack." Or *"He got hit by a car."* They're going: *"If I can't have this picture with this person, then I can't be happy."*

Well, that's not thinking. You're just remembering when you were happy and the person you're no longer with. They're not there anymore. You have to remember you're capable of going back to the memories you have, see what you saw when you enjoyed them, but you also have to see that they're gone.

What that really means is when you look into the future, you're capable of having good relationships. There are still 3.5 billion other people out there of the opposite sex – let alone of the same sex, which makes it 7 billion – that are possible people for you to enjoy your life with. Numerically, if your brain is looking for who you can enjoy and you already have examples of what that is, then you should be able to go out and move on.

My wife died after 30 years and there will never be another person like her. However, you can't find her, which is a shame because she was a great person. I had to find somebody who was completely different because if you try to replace somebody, that's not going to work. You can't look for what was, you have to look for what can be.

You have to think of the possibilities, know what you enjoy, and go after it as best you can. If you lose your job, you can't think of the life you used to have, you have to think of the life that's coming. I really enjoyed my kids when they were young. Then they started growing up on me. If you don't adapt to who they are now, you've got problems. I mean, my kids have kids! If you look at them and miss what was, and blow that out of proportion, you're not going to be able to move through things and adapt in a way where you look around and enjoy what's there.

If you eat in a restaurant and they serve you a bad meal, and you go back and order it again because you're familiar with the restaurant, people will go, *"That's stupid!"* However, it's no different than going into your brain and pulling up a thought that causes you great pain and leaving it the same size, the same distance, the same volume, running the same bad feelings.

If feelings feel bad and you keep running them in the same direction and looking at the same picture, it will go on. If you're paranoid and you keep making the same pictures of things that will scare you, you'll stay paranoid. That's all there is to it.

Now they tried to get rid of these things with drugs, electric shock treatment, everything under the Sun, but what we've got to do is teach people to think, and the younger we do it, the better off we'll be. We also have to teach people remembering is good, we just have to choose what we remember.

You need to remember words. If you're going to do something, take a word on paper and blow it up into a big picture of the word and remember the big picture, not the little one. It will be easier to see. If you're going to remember dates, you look at the list of dates, a big list and a big picture. If you want to memorize poetry or the lines of a play, you write it out in your head so it's huge.

You make it clear and focused, and you memorize it, look away, and go back. Then you can just read the thing and it'll be simple.

I remember watching the futurist Robert Anton Wilson sitting in a parking lot reciting a long poem. It was dark outside and we were waiting for a reservation in a restaurant. He was reciting this poetry, page after page. I was looking at him, going, *"How can you remember all of that?"* and he goes, *"I haven't thought about it in years, but when I think about it, it's as big as the sky out there."*

That's why he could recite poetry; when he looked at the poetry, he made the pages big in his mind and he read the words. They were easy to see. We taught people to have good memories, yet society spends too much time teaching people what to remember rather than giving them the machinery. If we taught people, *this* is remembering, *this* is thinking, *this* is calculating, they'd be much better off.

THE POWER OF CALCULATION

Calculation is a combination of both; you have to remember *how* things were done. If it works automatically, like multiplying, we'll get better results. Multiplication is not a conscious task; the machinery is in our brain. If someone asks you what's 5 x 5, you don't think about it, it pops out – 25! If we build those things in people's minds so we do it all the way up to 100 x 100, there's no combination of numbers people can't multiply. You add a few zeros and it won't make a difference.

It's not going to matter much if we build the machinery in so the memory works automatically, but we don't teach people to think on purpose. We tell them what to think, or things they could think, we even tell them what their thinking means, we analyze where it could have come from.

My simple solution to problems goes like this: They've got a bad memory they think about too much, I ask if it's life-size or larger-than-life. I go, *"There you go! If you think about this as a huge thing, it'll be a huge thing. Now shrink it down to the size of a silver dollar and blink it black and white. Now start at the end, play to the beginning really fast, and stick some circus music in there."* I do three or four different times, then I ask, "Does it make you feel bad now?" And they say no.

Typically, if there is a shrink in the room, they'll go, *"Yeah, but what if it comes back?"* I say, *"Well, it took five minutes to do, so six months from now you take another five minutes."* They go, *"Isn't there some problem underneath that's not being dealt with?"* Well, no. The problem was neurological, it happened automatically. We learn stuff, we neurologically code it, we build neuro-cortical pathways, and if we keep running the same ones, we will get the same results.

If we get a new phone number, for a while we keep dialing the old one. Eventually, though, your nervous system learns to do the new one first. It's not that you could never remember, I can hypnotize people and have them remember phone numbers from when they were five years old, but you don't need that. We keep putting new learnings on top of old ones.

We put layers and layers and layers on top of neuro-cortical pathways, billions of them. Be it ever so microscopic, they know which ones to run from the beginning to end and by size, chemically charging what's in there. If we run it backwards, we reduce the charge. If we reduce the adrenaline connected by reducing the size of the picture, if we give it somewhere else to go – which happens at a fraction of a millisecond – when it goes along that big charge, it won't stop. You won't get stuck.

You have to do something different. If you're in a state of rage, what you should do is take deep breaths and walk away and just say to yourself, *"I'm not going to be mad about this in 30 minutes."* Everybody's going to lose their temper every now and then, but when you're in the middle of rage, that's not the time to make decisions. You have to stop and look at yourself, or literally step out of the situation and say, *"Is this really that important?"* and just stop.

SMARTER LISTENING

In the world we live in today, we are getting bombarded with so many messages, ideas and theories that it's important to become smarter about knowing who to listen to. The old-fashioned way is the proof is in the pudding. To me, when I listen to people talk, they talk great theories, they're great motivational speakers, but the proof is they always have people giving testimonials. I'm always asking the question: Where are the rest of the people? They may have five people who give testimonials, but if they've got 3,000 in a room, I want to talk to all the rest of them and find out if this only worked on five people out of 3,000.

Probably, their advice is not what made it happen. Probably, the five people did something different from the rest. I want to know what the difference between them is. That's what modelers do. When I was first looking at modeling, I didn't listen to what these people said they were doing, I looked at the difference between when it worked and when it didn't in order to find out what to use for X and what to use for Y. I wanted to understand advice such as, *"Don't do this, do that!"*

When you're looking at it, whether we're designing pistol training courses or helicopter flying, the only thing you really care about is the stuff that works. A lot of people are all charged up about a theory, an idea, and they talk all about it. However, the big question is: *"What do you do on Monday morning? What are you going to do?"*

I want to see them do what they're actually talking about, I don't just want to hear about it. If you hear about something, you become a devotee. I see people like this all the time in cults and I see them in politics.

When you start asking people detailed questions about how you're going to handle real-world situations and they're promoting a political candidate, I go, *"Well, what are we going to do about this problem? How are we going to make the transition from this to that? What's going to happen?"* I'm listening to the answers.

We have had Obamacare in the United States and there are now so many regulations, it's ridiculous. There are all these coding things doctors have to put in to justify insurance payments. The books are so big that you could never memorize all the codes in there. There are millions of people sitting around making up all these rules and codes, and if you violate one of them, you could be fined $25,000. So, you have to hire an expert to be able to put the coding in.

We're moving medicine further and further away from the healthcare profession and more into the profession of being a servant of insurance companies. The people who believed this was a good idea didn't think far enough into the future and into the details to know what they were talking about. Everybody was emotionally invested in it – they were either against it or for it.

The truth is, something needed to be done. But as soon as it creates volumes, it's the wrong idea as far as I'm concerned. We need to be simplifying. We need to get rid of two laws for every one we pass so there are fewer laws, especially for things like the IRS. For every rule they add, we have to get rid of two or three rules so eventually it gets down to the point that it's comprehensible.

When you talk about comprehensive healthcare and affordable healthcare, there's a lot of stuff left out. What's going to make it affordable for everybody? How's it going to be paid for in the long-run? When that paying is done, how complicated is it going to be for the guy who's collecting the money? This is ultimately going to be the people providing the service. If you get to the point where a doctor cannot be in an office by himself seeing patients, it's a problem.

This is pretty much the way it is now - you can't be a doctor alone. Not only do you need a secretary, you need to have a computer system, and you have to go every three months to find out the new codes. You're going to be spending your time learning about coding instead of learning about new diseases and innovations in medicine. It's just not good use of time. We should be creating a system that gets doctors to be better doctors.

If you want cheaper healthcare, you build more medical schools and train people to be doctors. You create more nursing schools to make more nurses and more occupational therapists. We make the quality better and we teach people preventative health.

If we educated our kids in school in how to really exercise and made them like it, we would have fewer health problems. We have slightly better lunch programs now, but we have not put intelligence into these things, we have not put intelligence into designing the future. Everybody should be using *thinking* to design their future, and *memory* for what is was made for, remembering what not to do. But you shouldn't create things *not to do* and then not do them without having something better to do.

DAY 15
TASK

NAME IT

Notice whatever negative feeling you are experiencing and label it. Make yourself aware of the feeling and the fact that it's not necessarily the truth. Become aware of the stupidity of the negative feeling and how it fails to help you achieve what you want.

STOP IT

Notice what you are doing to engage in the negative feeling. Take the images and shrink them and white them out. Repeat the mantra to yourself *"Shut the fuck up"* or *"Stop it"* over and over again. Since feelings are created as a result of the images you make and the way you speak to yourself, it's important to make changes in these two dimensions to ensure that you feel differently.

TAKE A BREAK

Imagine the next time you start feeling intense negative feelings such as rage that you say to yourself *"Take a break"* or "It ain't that important" or *"Get over yourself."* Once you do this, instantly take a deep breath and get yourself out of the situation instantly. See yourself breaking the pattern and then asking the question: *"What do I want?"*

CHALLENGE AUTHORITY

Always consider who you are listening to and avoid believing any and every authority. Practice questioning their wisdom and learn to think for yourself. For example, if your friends are telling you that you'll never achieve your goals, ask yourself *"Have they ever been wrong?"* Practice being vigilant with who you listen to.

Thinking smarter really requires that you learn to think for yourself and embrace different perspectives. Practice and notice how these exercises help you to do just that.

CONCLUSION

In conclusion, we want you to start this whole process over again. If you spend each of these days doing this program, you will be able to change your life. You shouldn't be reading the book from cover to cover, you should go through those 15 days and practice them even more than once a day, even if it takes you a week.

It's not enough to do what's in a day, you have to *accomplish something* that day, you have to be able to adjust something you're not confident to do into something you are confident to do. Once you know how to do it, you'll always know how to do it. If you have something you have trouble motivating yourself to do, and you make yourself more motivated to follow the steps in how you get motivated, then you'll be more motivated.

After you have mastered the 15 days, you will have a solid beginning of what will make you smarter for the rest of your life. Luckily, after every 15 days, there's another 15 days, because you can always get more confident, you can always get more motivated, you can always find out things that make your body chemistry work better.

Fortunately, there are loads of magazines on these topics. There are lots of things coming out. If you don't add the right chemicals into your body, if you don't eat right, if you don't exercise, if you don't do the good things, good things don't happen.

A lot of people go on a diet and the minute they do the wrong thing, they go, *"The diet is over!"* The truth is, as far as I can tell almost every single diet works. The trouble is people stop. They lose 40lbs, they stop dieting, and they gain 40lbs back. Or they do the diet for two weeks and they lose 5lbs, then they have a night out and do all the wrong things and they feel terrible. They stop the diet and they gain more weight. What they don't do is go back to the beginning.

The thing is, from the time you're born to the time you die, you're either getting smarter or you're getting dumber. You don't really stay the same. That's not what happens, because as the world changes, you have to adapt to it.

If you're not adapting and becoming more motivated and more confident and making everything better, it'll get worse. For example, if you're not making your memory better, it gets worse. You may have memorized 20 words, but the world and knowledge in the world is exponentially changing. When you have to ask your kids how to work your cellphone, that's a good example of the world changing faster than you are.

There are things your cellphone will do and if you don't learn to do them, you're backing away from being smarter. The same thing is true of your computer or your television. I have a smart TV now. Now the TV has things on it I don't use because I don't want to. However, when you limit yourself because you don't learn what you need to, you have a problem.

Years ago, we didn't all own a computer. Only a few elite people knew how to run computers and they were very difficult to operate. It's constantly getting easier, but if we rely on the tools and not make our brains as smart as the machines, we'll have a problem.

If you lose your phone and that means you lose your friends because you don't know their phone numbers, that's not smart. The fact your phone can remember a number doesn't mean you shouldn't develop the ability to remember numbers. You want your memory to get better as you get older, not worse.

On our wedding day the first time I got married, everybody came up and told me how great sex was going to be at first and how it was going to disappear over time. That doesn't have to be the formula, because the truth is every year it kept getting better. Your golf game gets better over the years and it should. Everything else should as well. That's what smart is.

Smart is you keep learning, refining, adjusting and getting smarter. They say you'll eventually lose your memory; if you believe it's true, then you can make it happen. They're going to come up with ways of getting rid of Alzheimer's and getting rid of diseases. The amount of changes in medical science and the speed at which it's moving now is astronomical compared to what it was 100 years ago.

It used to be that people would say, *"It's as impossible as putting a man on the Moon!"* Well, we've been there and done that. The technology in your cellphone is more sophisticated than what took man to the Moon and back, computer-wise, and it is certainly a lot more condensed.

There were diseases that could never be cured and now they are eradicated. Death rates from cancer are diminishing, tuberculosis has almost disappeared, smallpox is almost completely eradicated and medical science will keep changing. Now, there's not as much thinking about curing diseases as preventing them. We're cracking genetic codes. The world is changing at a phenomenal rate, however people's minds aren't fast enough. Don't be one of those people.

This is the start of how to begin to go back through those 15 days and say, *"The first time through I kind of got it, I wonder if I can really refine it now."* Once you get through the 15 days, the big question is: What's next?

The smarter you become, the easier it is to live and the more you'll discover. The more I've learned about things, the more things there are for me to learn about. A very bright man said to me at the beginning of my career, *"You're having a creative burst. It'll last about six months so enjoy it because you'll be coasting on it forever."* That hasn't been my life. I even thought that was stupid then. I think the more I learn, the more questions you get answers to, the more questions there'll be. There's always a better way to go and that's not just with a machine like a cellphone. I'm sure the cellphones we have now are going to look ridiculous one day. I remember when cellphones were so big, if you looked at one now, it would look preposterous. We used to carry round these things with giant antennae sticking out of them. We thought they were miraculous. Now, we have things that fit in your pocket.

When I was a kid, phones were attached to the wall and had a handle you turned. The world of machines evolved at a great rate because people, in their minds, got smarter and figured out better ways to do things. That's not just a few scientists, that's all of us, all of us now know how to operate these things. It should also tell us that if you can have 300 channels on your TV, you can have 300 ideas in your mind.

If you believe there's only one way to motivate yourself or only one way to be confident, you'll get stuck. If you say the phrase, *"I'm the kind of person who…"* then you'll be frozen in time. You will be like one of those old people saying, *"If man were meant to fly, he'd have wings."* Guess what - he built wings and he flies everywhere! The truth is, you could be one of those smart people who does that. This is your chance to start becoming smarter on purpose by thinking on purpose. Now go ahead - and enjoy it!

ABOUT US

Dr. Richard Bandler

As Co-Creator of NLP, Dr. Bandler has for over 45 years dedicated himself to developing new ideas, new tools, new techniques and models for the advancement of human evolution. Richard Bandler's 30+ authored or co-authored books have sold millions of copies, and been translated into dozens of languages. Hundreds of thousands of people have studied with him to learn NLP, Design Human EngineeringTM, and neuro-hypnotic Re-PatterningTM. Richard Bandler has led the world into an era of behavioral technology.

Owen Fitzpatrick

Owen Fitzpatrick is an Globetrotting Psychologist and International Bestselling author who has been hired by Billionaires, Olympic athletes as well as the Coca Cola, Google, Salesforce, Pfizer, Oriflame, and Barclays Bank. Having traveled to more than 100 countries and spoken to audiences in more than 30 countries, he has authored 8 books which have been translated into more than 15 languages. Having co-founded the Irish Institute of NLP in 2001 with Brian Colbert, Owen became the youngest master trainer of NLP of all time in 2002. Owen's TEDx talk and YouTube videos have been viewed by more than a million people. Also an award winning actor and filmmaker, Owen's work has been screened in festivals in Europe and America. He has presented his own primetime television show for more than two years on RTE ONE, Irelands national television channel.

Dr. Glenda Bradstock

Dr. Glenda Bradstock has been helping people regain their health with Chiropractic care, Nutrition and Alternative therapies for the past 35 years. She graduated from Mills College with a BA in Philosophy. Then at Bank of America she worked in banking and finance until she had the opportunity to travel and produce a documentary film on the art, culture and religions of India and Nepal. From her career in photography she went back to school to become a Chiropractor and supervised other doctors and worked in her three practices in Texas. Dr. Bradstock continues to help people today as a Dream Builder Coach and Life Mastery Consultant.

WEBSITES

RichardBandler.com
PureNLP.com
NLPStore.com
DesignHumanEngineering.com
NeuroHypnoticRepatterning.com
NewThinkingPublications.com

PLUS
Owenfitzpatrick.com
Changingmindspodcast.com
NLP.ie
Onlinetimemastery.com
Charismatrainingacademy.com
Facebook.com/ofi23
Facebook.com/RealRichardBandler/
Twitter.com/rbandler
Twitter.com/owenfitzp
Youtube.com/owenjf23
Linkedin.com/in/owenfitzp/
Instagram.com/owenf23
Ancestrydna.com
23andme.com
Brainhq.com

FURTHER READING

Bandler, Richard

Using your Brain for a Change, Durango, CO, 1985

Magic in Action, New Thinking Publications, DE, 1985

Time for a Change, New Thinking Publications, DE, 1993

Get the life You Want, Harper Element, London, 2008

Make your life Great, Harper Element, London, 2010

Bandler, Richard, Delozier Judith and Grinder, John

Patterns of the Hypnotic Techniques of Milton H. Erickson, Volume 1, New Thinking Publications, DE, 1975

Bandler, Richard and Grinder, John

The Structure of Magic, New Thinking Publications, DE, 1975

The Structure of Magic, Volume 2, New Thinking Publications, DE, 1975

Transformations, Durango, CO, 1980

Frogs into Princes, New Thinking Publications, DE, 1979

Bandler, Richard and Benson, Kate

Teaching Excellence, New Thinking Publications, DE, 2017

Bandler, Richard and Fitzpatrick, Owen

Conversations with Richard Bandler, Health Communications, Deerfield Beach, FL, 2009

Memories, Hope is the Question, Mysterious Publications, Dublin, 2014

Bandler, Richard and La Valle, John,

Persuasion Engineering®, New Thinking Publications, DE, 1996

Bandler, Richard, Benson, Kate and La Valle, John, Fitzpatrick, Owen,Roberti, Alessio, Thomson, Garner, Mora, Alessandro, Piper, Anders

Seven Practical Applications of NLP, Attrakt, niewveen, 2012

Bandler, Richard, Thompson Garner

The Secrets of Being Happy, New Thinking Publications, DE, 2011

Colbert, Brian & Fitzpatrick, Owen

The Cynical Optimists, Truth be told media, 2018

D'Adamo Peter with Catherine Whitney

Eat Right 4 your Type, Penguin, 1997

Fitzpatrick, Owen;

The Charismatic Edge, Gill and MacMillan, 2013

Fitzpatrick, Owen

Not Enough Hours, Poolbeg Press, 2009

BOOKS FOR CHILDREN AND ADULTS TO SHARE

Bandler, Richard

The adventures of Anybody, New Thinking Publications, DE, 1993

Richard Bandler

Getting Smarter Series, Mental Clarity and More Mathematical Mind, CD

Richard Bandler

The Art and Science of nested loops, DVD

INDEX

A

B

C

D

263

J

JACKSON POLLOCK 141

K

L

LEARNED HELPLESSNESS 26, 27
LEGIONNAIRES DISEASE 19

M

MELANCHOLIA 53
MEMORIES 61, 62
MINERALS 223, 224
MOTIVATION 74, 95, 96, 101, 102, 103, 107, 113, 120, 139, 173, 174,
175, 176, 177, 178, 180, 181, 183, 185, 204, 252, 253

N

NEURO LINGUISTIC PROGRAMMING 20
NLP 20

O

OMEGA-3 221
OPTIMIZING 17, 20
OVEREATING 54, 55, 57, 58, 80, 93, 109, 111, 112, 114, 122, 123, 125,
176, 193, 197, 198, 201, 224, 252

P

PERSUASION ENGINEERING 70
PH LEVEL 225, 226
PHYSICISTS 141

Q

R

S

T

U

V

W

CPSIA information can be obtained
at www.ICGtesting.com
Printed in the USA
LVHW061443200519
618471LV00018BA/541/P

9 780998 716732